S0-BDQ-184

"*Seeing Yourself Through God's Eyes* is critical for every Christian to read to know what their relationship is to God."

—Dr. Robert S. McGee
Author, The Search for Significance

"*Seeing Yourself Through God's Eyes* is a dynamic devotional for both new and seasoned believers. It opens our eyes to the truth, focusing our attention on God's point of view of who we are in Christ."

—Vonette Z. Bright
Cofounder, Campus Crusade for Christ

"Telling yourself the truth about who you are in Christ will revolutionize your life. June shares the truth, based on the Word of God, to encourage and guide us in seeing ourselves through God's eyes. These foundational truths come alive in this study!"

—Barb Cline
Global Ambassador, HCJB Global

"'I am hidden with Christ'… 'I am chosen by God'…these and 29 more 'I am' statements—straight from God's Word—will encourage you to *stop* allowing false beliefs to dictate your self-image…and *start* seeing yourself through God's eyes."

—Nancy Epperson
President, Chesapeake-Portsmouth Broadcasting Corporation

"June Hunt has a unique way of exposing our emotions and then offering, through her words and genuine compassion, the healing that will follow. Just think what 31 days of her anointed biblically based perceptions could do for you if you were really willing to see yourself through God's eyes. Try it. It will change your life."

—H.B. London
Vice President, Focus on the Family

Seeing Yourself *Through*

GOD'S EYES

June Hunt

HARVEST HOUSE PUBLISHERS
EUGENE, OREGON

Unless otherwise indicated, Scripture quotations are taken from the Holy Bible, New International Version®, NIV®. Copyright © 1973, 1978, 1984, 2011 by Biblica, Inc.® Used by permission. All rights reserved worldwide.

Verses marked KJV are taken from the King James Version of the Bible.

Verses marked NASB are taken from the New American Standard Bible®, © 1960, 1962, 1963, 1968, 1971, 1972, 1973, 1975, 1977, 1995 by The Lockman Foundation. Used by permission. (www.Lockman.org)

Cover by Harvest House Publishers Inc., Eugene, Oregon

Cover photo © Pavelk / Shutterstock

SEEING YOURSELF THROUGH GOD'S EYES

Copyright © 2008 Hope for the Heart, Inc.
Published by Harvest House Publishers
Eugene, Oregon 97402
www.harvesthousepublishers.com

ISBN 978-0-7369-6457-9 (pbk.)
ISBN 978-0-7369-6458-6 (eBook)

All rights reserved. No part of this publication may be reproduced, stored in a retrieval system, or transmitted in any form or by any means—electronic, mechanical, digital, photocopy, recording, or any other—except for brief quotations in printed reviews, without the prior permission of the publisher.

Printed in the United States of America

15 16 17 18 19 20 21 22 23 / VP-JH / 10 9 8 7 6 5 4 3 2 1

When *both* a husband and wife live their lives reflecting their true identity in Christ, there is no more beautiful example of unity...no more inspiring display of God's design for marriage. Such is the case with

Beth and Bob Stapleton

What a joy to know a couple who long ago surrendered their lives to the Lord, trusting Him with their future. As a result, they have continually been conformed to the character of Christ. Despite inevitable trials, Bob and Beth's faith has grown stronger—and sweeter—with each passing year.

In this world, it is special to know even a handful of people whose lives so brightly radiate the love of God. But to know two, united in marriage, is a rare privilege.

I believe that here—and in heaven—there will continue to be a host of people who will say, "Beth and Bob, thank you for enriching our lives. We have consistently seen 'Christ in you, the hope of glory'" (Colossians 1:27).

Acknowledgments

With deepest appreciation to:

Pat McKay—for your delightful creativity…from day one

Sandy Menken—for typing each word…even through the night

June Page and Keith Wall—for your wise help…at the very last minute

Jill Prohaska and Angie White—for your finishing touches…always with a smile

And to my dear friend, Dorothy Patterson—no one has encouraged me more to write…and write…and keep on writing to present *God's truth for today's problems!*

"I pray that out of his glorious riches he may strengthen you with power through his Spirit in your inner being, so that Christ may dwell in your hearts through faith. And I pray that you, being rooted and established in love, may have power…to grasp how wide and long and high and deep is the love of Christ"
(Ephesians 3:16-18).

Contents

A Personal Word from June

Dear Friend,

Can you imagine what it would be like to be married...to exchange vows...to unite your hands and hearts? Now joined together as one, you and your bride drive to the airport, full of excitement about your honeymoon.

But before boarding the plane, you realize: *Oh no...my wallet!* Racing to return to the car, you yell, "I'll be back, honey—right back!"

She waits, and waits, and waits...until the plane leaves and your new bride is still left waiting. She's frantic now. After a thorough search of the airport and all known familiar spots, her new groom seems to have vanished!

Such is the true case of Sean McNulty, who was found three days later—wandering...disoriented...bug-bitten from head to toe. He didn't know his beloved Amy. He didn't know his own mother. He had amnesia—he didn't know his identity.

Identity. What would it be like to not know your own identity—to have *spiritual amnesia?* If you don't know who you are, you cannot experience deep inner peace and complete contentment—for instead, confusion reigns.

Sadly, this is how many people live today—they simply don't know who they are. But you do not have to live this way. The key is to learn to *see yourself through God's eyes.*

What if you simply don't know how God views you? The 31 daily devotions in this book will help you see your God-given worth and will remind you that, as a believer, *you are very special* in the heart and mind of the One who made you. Are you able to accept the truth that you have precious worth?

It might help to ask yourself, *How is the worth of an item established?* Let's assume you are at an auction. Item after item is presented for sale and item after item is sold—not always to the *same* bidder, but always to the *highest* bidder. To the one willing to pay the highest price.

Consider this: Jesus paid the ultimate price for you when He came to earth as a man, willingly died on the cross, and paid the penalty for your sins. Jesus Christ as God did not have to redeem you. But He loves you so much—you are so valuable to Him—He willingly paid the highest price.

Without a doubt, you have great worth in His eyes!

By meditating daily on the scriptures you read over the next 31 days, you will see your worth. As you train your mind to focus on the truth about yourself, your emotions will "be transformed by the renewing of your mind" (Romans 12:2).

In your heart, commit to faithfully do these spiritual exercises… take time to soak up all their truths. Then these Scripture passages will begin to saturate your heart, transform your thinking, and help develop the true picture of who you are…from God's point of view, the true point of view.

I want this to be an encouraging study for you! My prayer is that as you meet with God, you will take to heart His precious perspective of you. I pray that your emotions will be steadied and your heart will be secured because you will have begun to *see yourself through God's eyes.*

Yours in the Lord's hope,

June Hunt

What Is Your Identity?

Every person born into this world has had difficulty with identity at some time or another. All of us have struggled with our self-image.

Many spend a lifetime manipulating acceptance and attention from others, thinking they are building an indestructible tower of self-worth. Yet when people fail us and our logical expectations of our loved ones fall painfully short, our own self-worth can begin to crumble.

That's exactly the problem if we let our *identity be in another person*—we give that person too much control of us. And more so, we miss the vision God has of us and the immense value He places on us. The steps to understanding these truths are paved throughout Scripture. To tread these steps, we need to have a full understanding of what is meant by *identity*.

Have you ever asked yourself, *Who am I? Where am I going?* Do you understand your God-given worth? How essential to have accurate answers to these questions so that you can be what God created you to be and do what God created you to do.

Your Identity Determines Your Worth

Realize your *identity* ultimately determines your worth and your destination. In a very practical sense, if I were to enter a bank, step up to a teller, and say, "May I have $100?" the teller would ask for my account number or my name. If I had amnesia and didn't know who I was, I could not provide this information. And if I continued to request money, I would receive nothing but the directions to the front door.

However, knowing there are resources in my name—regardless of who placed them there—as long as I provide the teller with my name and account number, I can quickly receive the cash requested. My *identity* definitely determines my *worth* and my ability to draw upon that reserve.

Your Identity Determines Your Destination

What about your destination? *Where are you going?*

Some time ago I planned to fly from Dallas to Atlanta to speak at a convention and arrived at the airport with time to spare. Prior to the final boarding call, I made a quick phone call, using the extra time I thought I had. When I began to board, I was told they had started assigning seats for standby passengers and I should have checked in at the main desk (mistakenly, I thought the boarding pass in my hand was sufficient...but my seat might have been given to someone else).

My heart raced as I approached the agent at the desk and handed him my ticket. Would I be allowed to leave? A silent eternity passed as he scanned a computer screen for the official flight passenger list.

He checked for my name, saw it, and said with a smile, "Yes, you are on this flight. You may board the plane." Indeed, my *identity* was directly linked to the *destination* of that plane.

Much more critical is our identity in terms of ultimate worth and eternal destination. The Bible states there are two different "identities" or "families" for all human beings: those who are *in Adam*, and those who are *in Christ*. First Corinthians 15:21-22 says, "Since death came through a man, the resurrection of the dead comes also through a man. For as in Adam all die, so in Christ all will be made alive."

The question is this: *To which of these two families do you belong?* Your personal identification with one of these families will determine your characteristics and your inheritance.

Your Identity Determines Your Characteristics

Our physical characteristics are determined by our biological families. In college, my freshman roommate was Josephine Eng from Hong Kong. She had straight black hair, dark brown eyes, a dark complexion, flattened features, and a small frame. In stark contrast, I had curly blond hair, green eyes, a fair complexion, angular features, and a large frame.

No matter how much time I spent with Josephine, I could never possess her characteristics. Simply put, I could not have Eng characteristics unless I had been born into the Eng family. Likewise, when we were born into the family of Adam, we *inherited characteristics* from his family line.

Since Adam made the choice in the Garden of Eden not to obey God, he and all his descendants are "identified" with sin (this is their *identity*). This heart of independence is the basic *nature* we have all inherited. Psalm 51:5 says, "Surely I was sinful at birth, sinful from the time my mother conceived me." Consequently, our *natural inclination* is to sin because we are born of Adam's family.

Your Identity Determines Your Inheritance

However, since God made it possible for us to change families, we are able to receive a new identity—*a new nature!* You can be "adopted" into the family of Christ and become a child of God. Then you lose your identity in Adam and receive your identity in Christ. As a result, you receive your *new characteristics.* The Bible says, "If anyone is in Christ, he is a new creation; the old has gone, the new has come!" (2 Corinthians 5:17).

Your old natural *sin nature* is supernaturally changed for a new *divine nature* (2 Peter 1:3-4). A consequence of this new identity is a *new worth* based on the abundant resources placed into your personal account. A second consequence is a *new destination* throughout eternity, where you will forever be secure in the presence of God.

Precious one, how God desires that you will receive all that He provides! The struggle with low-self-worth can be replaced with godly self-worth when you are in Christ. But in order for you to have the characteristics of Christ, *you must be in a different family.*

Has that change become a reality for you? If not, on the authority of the Word of God, you can become a child of God. The Bible says, "To all who received him [Jesus], to those who believed in his name, he gave the right to become children of God" (John 1:12).

If you desire this new relationship with God through Christ, you can pray this prayer:

> *God, I want a real relationship with You. I admit, many times I have chosen wrong. I know I've sinned, and I'm asking You to forgive me for my sins. I now want to become a child of God. Jesus, thank You for dying on the cross for my sins—for shedding Your blood on the cross to pay the price I should have paid.*
>
> *Come into my life to be my Lord and my Savior. I yield my will to Your will. Thank You for loving me. Thank You for forgiving me. Thank You for giving me the free gift of eternal life. Lord, make me the person You created me to be. In Your holy name I pray, Amen.*

If you sincerely prayed that prayer in true humility, you can thank God for His heart's desire to move you into a new family—*His family.* How extraordinary—every child of God genuinely has a new worth, a new destination, and a new identity! Now you can begin to see yourself through God's eyes!

Your New Life in Christ

"For as in Adam all die, so in Christ all will be made alive" (1 CORINTHIANS 15:22).	
"For as in Adam all die…	**so in Christ all will be made alive."**
In Adam	*In Christ*

In Adam		In Christ	
Old creation	2 Corinthians 5:17	New creation	2 Corinthians 5:17
Hardened heart	Ezekiel 36:26	New heart	Ezekiel 36:26
Death	Ezekiel 36:2	Life	Romans 6:22
Powerless	Romans 5:6	Power	1 Peter 1:3
Enemies of God	Romans 5:10	Reconciled to God	Romans 5:10
Condemned	Romans 5:6	No condemnation	Romans 8:1
Slave	Galatians 4:7	Son	Galatians 4:7
Slave to sin	Romans 6:6	Free from sin	Romans 6:7
Slave to impurity	Romans 6:19	Slave to righteousness	Romans 6:19
Poverty	2 Corinthians 8:9	Riches	2 Corinthians 8:9
Accused	Colossians 1:22	Blameless	Colossians 1:22
Under law	Romans 6:14	Under grace	Romans 6:14
Under judgment	Romans 5:16	Justified	Romans 5:16
Under a curse	Galatians 3:13	Redeemed from curse	Galatians 3:13
Under wrath	Ephesians 2:3	Free from wrath	Romans 5:9
In the darkness	Ephesians 5:8	In the light	Ephesians 5:8

Discovering How God Sees You

"If you call out for insight and cry aloud for understanding, and
if you look for it as for silver and search for it as for hidden
treasure, then you will...find the knowledge of God"

(PROVERBS 2:3-5).

Y ou are about to unearth the most priceless of all hidden treasures.
To begin this great discovery, all you need is a pen, paper, and
your favorite Bible translation. As you bring to the surface the truths
of each daily devotion, you will see God's perspective of you from His
Word.

Research[1] has shown that it takes three weeks to form a habit;
therefore, as you end this study, you should be in the precious process
of *seeing yourself through God's eyes.* The following six steps will be used
by the Spirit of God to bring to light that which may be currently
hidden from view:

1. Begin each day asking God to reveal how He sees you...
   simply because you are His child.

2. Concentrate on the initial statement concerning you and on
   the corresponding scripture.

3. Read the practical commentary and pray that the Lord's
   heavenly view of you would penetrate your heart.

4. Look up the additional Scripture passages in your Bible,
   then personalize and paraphrase them, putting them into
   your own words.

5. Write a personal prayer and complete the phrase, "Father,
   through Your eyes I can see that I _____."

6. Repeat to yourself the truth printed at the bottom of the

page. With a grateful heart, acknowledge that you have infinite worth in the eyes of your heavenly Father.

Day 32

I Am Given the Compassion of Christ

Personalize these verses in your own words:

Isaiah 49:15 _No matter who rejects me, the Lord will never forget me. No matter who is cold toward me, the Lord has compassion for me, even greater than a mother for her child._

Lamentations 3:22-23 _God not only loves me, He also has great compassion for me. I don't need to be overcome by my trials because God will always love me and be faithful to me._

Father, through Your eyes I can see that I... _will never be without Your love and compassion. I shouldn't base how I feel about myself on how I am being treated by others. Thank You that Your compassion will never fail me._

I am loved because...I have the unfailing compassion of Christ.

Part 1

MY POSITION IN CHRIST

"How great is the love the Father has lavished on us, that we should be called children of God!"

(1 JOHN 3:1).

Day 1

I Am Adopted by God

"He predestined us to be adopted"
(EPHESIANS 1:5).

Oh, to be secure! Everyone wants it; everyone longs for it. Why? Perhaps *security* has added significance to us because we all know the feeling of having the proverbial "rug pulled out from under us" by someone we trusted. At one time we felt at home in the relationship, but rejection sent us out the door and into the pit of abandonment.

Is there a place you can call "home" and not question its permanence? A place of emotional security—a place that will last throughout eternity? Consider what your heavenly Father has said: "I have adopted you."

Even though God already has a Son, He chooses to adopt you. God does not *have* to adopt you; He *wants* to! You are His child; He is your loving Father.

Thomas Watson expressed it this way: "Since God has a Son of His own, and such a Son, how wonderful God's love in adopting us! We needed a Father, but He did not need sons."[2]

If you have not had a meaningful relationship with your earthly father, it may be hard for you to fully comprehend a caring, loving heavenly Father. Unlike some earthly fathers, God is always available to you. He will neither leave you nor forsake you—He is with you all the time. He desires to be intimately involved in every aspect of your life. By adopting you, He has chosen you to have the full privilege of being His own.

Many similarities can be seen between God's adoption of us and the legal adoption of a child. An adopted child is not inferior to any other child in the family. Adopted children carry the family name, and their inheritance is secure because they, too, are legal heirs.

However, there is one difference between legal adoption and God's adoption: A legally adopted child will not receive the same nature as the newly adoptive parents, who have different biological genes and characteristics. Yet when you are adopted by God, you always receive a new nature—the nature of your heavenly Father.

History tells us that when the New Testament was written, it was understood an adoption could never be revoked. Do you realize what that means in light of your relationship with God? *Once you are selected, you can never be rejected.* You will never be emotionally abandoned. You will always have a home in God's heart. Seeing yourself through God's eyes, you are His child *forever*.

Personalize these verses in your own words:

Romans 8:15 _____
_____
_____
_____
_____

Galatians 4:5-7 _____
_____
_____
_____
_____

Father, through Your eyes I can see that I... _____
_____
_____
_____
_____

I am secure because...I am adopted by God.

I Am a Child of God

*"How great is the love the Father has lavished on us,
that we should be called children of God!"*

(1 JOHN 3:1).

What a tender scene...Jesus with the children! His disciples felt they were a nuisance, yet Jesus recognized their needs and was eager to place His hands on them and pray for them. "Let the little children come to me, and do not hinder them, for the kingdom of heaven belongs to such as these" (Matthew 19:14).

Perhaps you experienced an unhappy childhood and grew up in a situation where you felt unloved. Such an experience can profoundly affect your life—even as an adult—and can result in a long, continuing search for love and acceptance.

Perhaps you've felt like a nuisance, unwanted and unwelcomed. It is no small matter that your heavenly Father calls you His child, a loving term of endearment. Dear child of God, you *are* loved, you *are* wanted, and you *do* belong. The very "longing to belong" is put in your heart by God Himself. He creates a desire in your heart to know Him as your loving Father.

You may have heard people say, "Everyone is a child of God." While this sounds warm and wonderful, it is simply not true! According to John 1:12, "To all who received him [Jesus Christ], to those who believed in his name, he gave the right to become children of God."

While the Bible teaches that everyone on earth is a *creation* of God, only those who *receive* Jesus as Lord and Savior become authentic children of God.

If a teenager you had never seen before strolled into your house, headed for the refrigerator, made a sandwich, and plopped down on your sofa, what would you do? How long would you permit this intruder to continue this pretentious behavior? Not long!

Yet if your own child walked in, headed for the refrigerator, made a sandwich, and so forth, you wouldn't think anything about it. Because the child belongs there, he has a right to the comforts of home. As a part of your family, he has family privileges.

The same is true for you as a child of God…you are part of His family. He delights in providing for your needs, and as His child, you can look to Him to meet your needs. You can come into His presence at any time. Seeing yourself through God's eyes, you are welcomed, you are wanted.

You are "at home" in God's family.

Personalize these verses in your own words:

Romans 8:16 _____
_____
_____
_____

Ephesians 2:19 _____
_____
_____
_____

Father, through Your eyes I can see that I… _____
_____
_____
_____

I am secure because…I am a child of God.

Day 3

I Am Precious to God

"You are precious and honored in my sight, and...I love you"
(ISAIAH 43:4).

Does anyone care? Do I make a difference in anyone's life? Do I matter at all?

When the answers seem bleak, it's important to realize that although few have escaped the painful rocks of rejection, a shipwrecked soul is not at the heart of God's plan for any child of His. When trials seem unending, when heartaches are hitting wave upon wave, if only we could remember, *This too will pass.* God says, "You are precious and honored in My sight."

Do you feel precious to God? Do you consider yourself cherished? Even when you feel you are not, *you truly are.* Though at times you've been drenched with defeat, God's love is like the endless tide.

Your compassionate Savior wants you to "know that the testing of your faith develops perseverance. Perseverance must finish its work so that you may be mature and complete, not lacking anything" (James 1:2-4).

One of life's most beautiful and costly wonders is born out of pain and irritation. When a grain of sand slips through the opening of an oyster's shell, the oyster immediately begins to cover the sand with a substance that eventually develops into one of the world's exquisite gems—a lovely, luminous pearl. The larger the oyster and the greater the irritation, the larger the pearl and greater the value.

Perhaps a "grain of sand"—an excruciating trial—is causing you painful irritation right now. Remember God has not abandoned you. He has a purpose in allowing trials to invade your life. God's plan for you is perfect—to produce a pearl of great value.

Even in the midst of a storm, you are safe. Your Savior will protect you from the storm's destruction.

Jeremy Taylor wrote, "We are as safe at sea, safer in the storm which God sends us, than in a calm when we are befriended with the world."[3]

Trials are purposeful. God can use them to produce in you qualities that could not be cultivated in any other way. As you see yourself through God's eyes, know you are of great value to Him and He desires the very best for you. He says, "You are precious and honored in My sight, and…I love you."

Personalize these verses in your own words:

Isaiah 43:2 _____

_____

_____

_____

_____

Jeremiah 29:11 _____

_____

_____

_____

_____

Father, through Your eyes I can see that I… _____

_____

_____

_____

_____

I am secure because…I am precious in the sight of God.

I Am Accepted by God

"He hath made us accepted in the beloved [Jesus]"
(Ephesians 1:6 kjv).

Many people have a recording in their minds playing the same song over and over again. The title? *If Only.* The air play? *Top 10!* Not just for weeks, but for years. The most distinguishing feature of this song is its brevity—only one line long. "If only _____, then I might have pleased my dad." "If only…I had been smarter in school." "If only…I had been better in sports." "If only…I had been more like my brother." "If only…I had been born first." "If only…I had not been born at all!"

All through our lives, this one-line song continues to play. We even remember the ones from our earliest childhood experiences and keep rehearsing them…an indicator that we are emotionally stuck.

The child who hears, "You'll never amount to anything" will struggle with self-worth. The child who hears, "I wish you had never been born" becomes performance-based throughout life, trying to prove some sense of importance to everyone. Perhaps the perceived "If it weren't for you, I'd be happy" theme is the most melancholy melody of all. This kind of rejection ravages the heart of a child…of any age.

Dr. Charles Stanley says most of us value the acceptance of our parents more than any other person. He cites businessmen in their forties, fifties, and even sixties who are still seeking their father's acceptance and approval…even though their fathers are dead. The little boy inside still cries out, *I've got to get my dad to accept me.*

While we all make mistakes, in God's eyes you are no mistake. As a child of God, you are never unacceptable to Him. He says, "Never will I leave you; never will I forsake you" (Hebrews 13:5).

Jesus understands your innermost feelings when you've been

rejected. He personally experienced the same kind of rejection from His family. "He came unto his own, and his own received him not" (John 1:11 KJV). Therefore, who can better empathize with your need for acceptance than your Lord!

Be absolutely assured God never looks at you and says, "If only..." He loves and accepts you, period...just as you are. When you see yourself through God's eyes, you will exchange those old, warped, worn-out melodies of self-condemnation for the simple but classic refrain:

> Jesus loves me! This I know, for the Bible tells me so...
> Jesus loves me! He will stay close beside me all the way.[4]

Personalize these verses in your own words:

Psalm 27:10 _____

_____

_____

_____

_____

Jeremiah 31:3 _____

_____

_____

_____

_____

Father, through Your eyes I can see that I... _____

_____

_____

_____

_____

I am secure because...I am accepted in the beloved.

I Am Called by Name by God

"I have summoned you by name; you are mine"
(ISAIAH 43:1).

Have you ever arrived at an airport, train station, or special event and found no one was there to welcome you…to call you by name? Have you ever rushed home with anxious anticipation to share exciting news only to find an empty house and a deafening silence? In the depths of your being you have a need to feel you are personally known, lovingly cared about, and personally called by name.

Even though it had been several months since I had spoken and sung at a particular Christian retreat, the stinging comments from one significant person had produced acute pain. I was still smarting, as if from a bee sting. When you are stung by a bee, the sting catches you by surprise—the stinger remains, the swelling begins, the skin reddens, and the surrounding area becomes sensitive to touch. My heart felt that same painful sensitivity as I planned to fly back to the location of the retreat. Although mentally I had been preparing myself for the return, I still had a full-blown case of fear—fear I would be hurt again.

A week prior to my departure, I mailed a note to someone who had been especially concerned about me during my time of hurt. I didn't ask her to pick me up, but I did include my flight schedule with the hope she would read between the lines and be there upon my arrival.

As I deplaned, my eyes searched the airport waiting area for that one familiar face. I wanted to hear a warm, "Hi, June!" but only the drone of a swarming crowd echoed in my ears. Even though I had tried to prepare myself, my heart sank.

Starting toward the baggage area, I suddenly heard a voice…someone called out my name…"June!" Thank You, Lord, she was there! She had been on the observation deck long before the plane had arrived.

And now she was calling me by name. Her considerate and concerned voice, her presence, all communicated, "I care about you." Her coming acted as a healing balm to soothe my not-yet-healed heart.

When situations in your life begin to sting, don't assume God has forgotten you. He is still watching over you. As you see yourself through God's eyes, realize your Lord is always there. He is always intimately involved in your life. You are constantly on His mind. He says, "Fear not...I have [called] you by name; you are mine."

> *He who counts the stars, and calls them by their names,*
> *is in no danger of forgetting His own children. He knows*
> *your case as thoroughly as if you were the only crea-*
> *ture He ever made, or the only saint He ever loved.*[5]
> —CHARLES HADDON SPURGEON

Personalize these verses in your own words:

Psalm 139:13-16 _____

_____

_____

_____

_____

Father, through Your eyes I can see that I... _____

_____

_____

_____

_____

I am secure because...I am called by name by God.

I Am Baptized with Christ

*"We were therefore buried with him
through baptism into death"*
(Romans 6:4).

The little girl had no one with whom she could identify. She wanted to find her family, but didn't know how. She searched with all her might.

> Somewhere over the rainbow
> Way up high,
> There's a land that I heard of
> Once in a lullaby...[6]

In 1939, millions of people flocked to see the unveiling of the first motion picture to be filmed in both black and white and living color. *The Wizard of Oz* featured colors woven throughout the fabric of the story. The motion picture industry would never be the same—this rainbow of colors gave it an exciting new identity.

In a similar way, one who is baptized in Christ will never be the same. The word *baptism* is black and white for many people, clearly understood and recognized as a vital step of obedience in their Christian walk. To others, its image has become a muddy gray...a convoluted mixture of misunderstood concepts and misapplied doctrine. Yet when you correctly understand the meaning of *baptizo*, the New Testament Greek verb for "baptize," you will see a panorama of living color unfold before your very eyes.

For centuries, when people immersed a piece of cloth (Greek, *baptizo*) into a dye, that resulted in a change of identity. A bland muslin fabric would be transformed into a brilliant blue or radiant red cloth suitable for any number of important uses.

Do you realize when you were "buried with Christ through

baptism," you actually received a *change of identity?* Although you are still made of the same material, your new identity with Christ permeates the very fabric of your soul and spirit.

Your *spiritual* baptism takes place the moment you are saved, as you are instantaneously identified with Christ. Later, *water* baptism takes place as an outward symbol of what has happened inside you.

Your water baptism symbolizes a progression of three pictures:

- Standing in the water represents your old life.
- Being lowered under the water represents the death and burial of your old life—the washing away of your sins.
- Being lifted up out of the water represents your new life in Christ.

You are now baptized into Christ, and you are lifted into a colorful new life...into a new family...into a *new identity.* All about you is new!

Personalize these verses in your own words:

Galatians 3:26-27 _____

_____

_____

_____

Colossians 2:9-12 _____

_____

_____

_____

Father, through Your eyes I can see that I... _____

_____

_____

_____

I am secure because...I am now identified with Christ.

I Am Hidden with Christ

"You are my hiding place; you will protect me from trouble"
(PSALM 32:7).

The Nazis wielded terror over all who were not like them in race, religion, or rule. During World War II, the primary target of hate was the Jews: Their power stripped, property confiscated, people confined—and killed—in concentration camps. In Nazi-dominated Holland, the ten Boom family had carefully hidden hundreds of Jews in their "hiding place"—a secret place in their home above their watch shop.

Then on February 28, 1944, what they feared most happened—the hiding place was discovered! The Gestapo arrested the ten Boom family. Their crime? Hiding Jews. Their punishment? Immediate transport to a concentration camp.

As two of the sisters in the ten Boom family (Corrie and Betsie) waited in line to be searched, Corrie asked God if He would keep the Bible tucked inside her clothing hidden from view. "Dear God…You have given me this precious Book; You have kept it hidden through checkpoints and inspections." The woman in front of Corrie was searched three times. Corrie's beloved sister, Betsie, standing behind her, was also searched. Miraculously, the officer never touched Corrie. Her Bible now had a hiding place in a German concentration camp![7]

Filth, disease, beatings, and rape became a part of their struggle for survival. Many probably became embittered toward their captives. But as God spoke to Corrie through the Bible, she knew His Word would keep hatred from her heart. "I have hidden your word in my heart that I might not sin against you" (Psalm 119:11).

Is there a hiding place for you? A place of healing for your damaged emotions? When you have been treated harshly, you can be free of hatred. Because God hides His truth in you, you are protected from wrong thoughts and choices. The adversary of your life has no power to trap you as long as you stay hidden in the shelter of God's wings, where you are safe from emotional destruction, hidden from emotional ruin.

The ten Boom family had their hiding place but only for a brief while. As God's child, you are hidden in Christ, and by seeing yourself through God's eyes, you can know you are safe forever!

> Under His wings, what a refuge in sorrow!
> How the heart yearningly turns to His rest!
> Often when earth has no balm for my healing,
> There I find comfort and there I am blest.[8]

Personalize these verses in your own words:

Psalm 17:8 _____

_____

_____

_____

_____

Colossians 3:3 _____

_____

_____

_____

_____

Father, through Your eyes I can see that I... _____

_____

_____

_____

I am secure because...I am hidden with Christ.

Part 2

GOD'S PLAN FOR ME

"'Come now, let us reason together,' says the LORD.
'Though your sins are like scarlet, they shall be
as white as snow; though they are red as
crimson, they shall be like wool'"
(ISAIAH 1:18).

Day 8

I Am Chosen by God

"He chose us in him before the creation of the world"
(EPHESIANS 1:4).

School was in session, and everything was fine...fine until it was time for teams to be chosen. As the team captains called out the names of their chosen players, the air filled with awkwardness—at least for one timid teenager who was anything but agile. *Oh God, I hate being chosen last. Please, let somebody want me!*

Have you ever longed to be chosen because you were really wanted, because you were really desired? Child of God, the Lord chose you "before the creation of the world." He chose you because He *wanted* you—not because of your strength, scholarship, or skill. You can take no credit or merit in being chosen. Jesus clearly states, "You did not choose me, but I chose you" (John 15:16).

Many years ago, another child found himself in a situation of being chosen. The Lord sent the prophet Samuel to Jesse of Bethlehem, saying, "I have chosen one of his sons to be king" (1 Samuel 16:1). What an unfathomable honor for a family! Yet after Samuel had surveyed Jesse's seven sons, he said, "The LORD has not chosen these... Are these all the sons you have?" (1 Samuel 16:10-11). Well, there was David, the youngest. But he was away tending sheep—and he certainly was not "king material"! At the prophet's insistence, however, the lad was brought in. Immediately the Lord told Samuel to choose David, "and from that day on the Spirit of the LORD came upon David in power" (1 Samuel 16:13).

Later, in a most critical battle we see the giant Goliath completely terrorizing the army of Saul, king of Israel. However, God uses the young, inexperienced David as the man of the hour. Imagine the Israelites' amazement as they watched David, without armor, approaching

Goliath. Just how could this young man be confident of conquest? David knew this simple principle: Whatever God *chooses* for you to do, He will *equip* you to do. In a moment, David single-handedly slew the nine-foot-tall titan. His secret? He understood the true source of strength, declaring before the confrontation, "The battle is the LORD's" (1 Samuel 17:47).

What truth for you today! When you face the "Goliaths" in your life, remember this: You have been chosen *by* the Lord. As you now see yourself through God's eyes, have confidence *in* the Lord—the battle is the Lord's!

Personalize these verses in your own words:

John 15:19 _____

_____

_____

_____

_____

Romans 8:33 _____

_____

_____

_____

_____

Father, through Your eyes I can see that I… _____

_____

_____

_____

_____

I have confidence because…I am chosen by God.

I Am Born Again by God

"You must be born again"
(JOHN 3:7).

No sentence in Scripture has been subjected to more contemporary cynicism, sarcasm, and satire than the impossible-sounding, "You must be born again." Born again? Jesus left no other option. He said it is a must! But why?

In God's original creation, Adam and Eve were made in the image of God. The Lord told them they could eat from any tree except for one, or they would die. So what did they do? They took a bite of that forbidden fruit—and what a bitter aftertaste!

They were immediately expelled from their life in the garden paradise. And some might wonder, *But why didn't they die?* Obviously their bodies didn't die, nor did their souls (their personalities). But they became spiritually dead. Likewise, all who were born after them were born dead in their sins.

Upon your physical birth you were born with a sin nature (Psalm 51:5). You were born lost, alienated, spiritually dead. What is the only thing a dead person needs? Life! Not sincerity or education, culture or finances, or even religion. When you are dead, you need life.

Spiritually, when you accept Christ, the Savior, to live inside you, you go from death to life. You receive Christ's life! As a result, you are given a new nature—His nature. And you are given a new spirit—His Spirit.

The phrase "born again," in the New Testament Greek text, literally means "born anew, born from above." When the Spirit of God so transforms a life, it can only be described as a dramatic new birth. Oh, child of God, marvel at the beauty of being *born from above!*

The critic says, "Impossible! How can a person be born again?" Yet in nature, God has given us the little caterpillar to unravel this mystery for the whole world to see. This drab and dull creature worms its way through life until it dies to its caterpillar existence. Then the impossible occurs: The death of the caterpillar brings forth the birth of the butterfly. Behold—the miracle of the monarch! A two-inch worm unfolds to become a creature with a four-inch wingspan. A pallid, pale green is transformed into a regal, reddish gold. A former creeping crawler becomes airborne and is enabled to make a migratory trip of nearly 2,000 miles in flight!

So it is when you are born anew that you can see yourself through God's eyes. The old is gone, and the new is alive—to soar to heights unknown.

Now, spread your wings, child of God...soar to new heights!

Personalize these verses in your own words:

2 Corinthians 5:17 _____
_____
_____
_____

1 Peter 1:3,23 _____
_____
_____
_____

Father, through Your eyes I can see that I... _____
_____
_____
_____

I have confidence because...I am born anew by God.

I Am Saved by God

"It is by grace you have been saved, through faith—
and this not from yourselves, it is the gift of God"
(EPHESIANS 2:8).

My brother's family was excited about moving into their new home. The carpet was down, the curtains were up, the furniture was in. Only a few items remained to be moved. Then in the early morning just before the family was to take up residence, a fire broke out, and their possessions went up in flames. Personal items, precious mementos, and priceless pictures were all lost.

When I arrived at the charred frame, I had expected to see my brother. Instead, he and his family had gone to the homes of two firemen who, to my horror, had lost their lives in the blaze. The cry of all our hearts was, If only they could have been saved! Only against such a black backdrop could the significance of salvation become so desperately real.

Saved...who wouldn't want to be saved? The word *saved* obviously implies being saved *from* something. Oh, if only all humanity would comprehend what Scripture says they can be saved from: an eternal existence of complete anguish, a destiny of living in darkness. Who wouldn't want deliverance?

Just think: As a Christian, you were delivered from this dominion of darkness. In the New Testament, the Greek word for *saved* means "to be delivered, to be preserved." This is the eternal benefit resulting from your decision to accept Christ's offer of salvation.

But the scope of spiritual salvation doesn't extend just to being saved from the *penalty* of sin. As a child of God, you are also saved from the *power* of sin. You are actually "dead to sin" (Romans 6:11). Simply put, you can break free from any sinful habit! And that's not all. One day, in heaven, you will be saved from the very *presence* of sin.

For me, the most phenomenal aspect of salvation is not what we've been saved *from,* but rather what we've been saved *for.* God's desire is not just to get us *out* of hell, but to get the Savior *into* us...not just to rescue us from eternal death, but to conform us into the likeness of our Rescuer, Jesus Himself.

With His presence in you, you have His power, His wisdom, His forgiveness, His love, and His strength. It is His life *in* you, living His life *through* you!

What incredible value! And the amazing fact is that it's a free gift. But it's not cheap. It cost Christ His life. Salvation is a free gift to you and me because Christ paid for it and you now can see yourself, your immense value, through God's eyes.

Personalize these verses in your own words:

Exodus 15:2 _____

_____

_____

_____

_____

Hebrews 7:25 _____

_____

_____

_____

_____

Father, through Your eyes I can see that I... _____

_____

_____

_____

_____

I have confidence because...I am saved by God's grace.

I Am Justified by God

"You were justified in the name of the Lord Jesus Christ"
(1 CORINTHIANS 6:11).

Have you ever been on trial? There you stand, in life's courtroom of criticism and accusation. Devastated, you face enemies sitting in the role of judge and jury. How is it others can have such control over events shaping your life? How can you deal with the pain of unwarranted faultfinding and unjustified conclusions? What is your position when you are condemned and determined to be guilty by these self-appointed critics?

The most extraordinary day of your Christian life is the day when you are on trial. Your rightful Judge brings down the gavel and proclaims you *justified*. God uses a legal term that means, "acquitted, vindicated, declared righteous." A popular amplification for *justified* is *just-as-if-I'd* never sinned.

Imagine yourself in a court of law. The judge has heard the testimony of the highway patrol officer. He has determined you are guilty of speeding, and firmly pronounces a mandatory fine of $100. Then a most unexpected thing happens, causing a stir in the courtroom. The judge rises, steps down from the bench, and takes off his robe. Opening his wallet, he counts out the correct currency and pays your fine! This judge happens to be your father. As a judge, he must make sure justice is served as he applies the law of the land to your actions. But as a father, he demonstrates the love in his heart, pays your penalty, and buys your freedom.

This scene portrays what your heavenly Father did for you. As a *just* God, He has to sentence you to death because of your sins. But as a *loving Father,* He provided the payment for your sins—and you received life. Jesus was the payment. His death bought you life. His death paid the price.

When you yield control of your life to Christ, you are more than pardoned. A pardoned sinner is simply excused from the penalty of sin, but the charge is still recorded. However, when you are justified by God, you receive total acquittal not only from all obligation, but also from all accusation! The charge is erased from your record in the book of life. On every charge brought against you, the Judge has spoken, and no one can reverse His divine decision. As you see yourself through God's eyes, you realize you are acquitted, vindicated, and justified!

Personalize these verses in your own words:

Romans 5:1 _____
_____
_____
_____
_____

Galatians 2:16 _____
_____
_____
_____
_____

Father, through Your eyes I can see that I… _____
_____
_____
_____
_____

I have confidence because…I am justified by God.

I Am Redeemed by God

"Christ redeemed us"
(GALATIANS 3:13).

In March of 1932, the entire world grieved with the Charles Lindbergh family when their 20-month-old son was kidnapped. Little Charles, Jr. was abducted from his home and held for $50,000 ransom. Aviator Lindbergh had become an international hero after making the first transatlantic flight in 1927. However, his fame did not protect his child from danger. Neither did it protect him from the desperate desire to pay the ransom. Yet even with the full ransom paid, the Lindberghs found themselves victimized, powerless to change the evil travesty. Their baby was cruelly killed by the kidnapper.

The world's first abduction was carried out in a garden setting. Eden was the perfect haven provided by God for the first man and woman, Adam and Eve. With cunning cleverness, the adversary-kidnapper, Satan, tempted and lured the innocent pair into sin and thereby made hostages of all who were to follow. Alienated from home and sentenced to separation from God and to death, the only hope for the human race was "to be released on receipt of the ransom."

Unlike the Lindberghs, who could not save their child, the heavenly Father sent His Son, Jesus Christ, to *redeem* you—His child—by paying the full ransom with His life. His death purchased your life! The price? His shed blood.

The two New Testament Greek verbs translated *redeemed* mean "to release on receipt of a ransom" or "to buy out." Bible scholar Lawrence Richards explains that *redeemed* is set "against the background of helplessness...human beings captured, held captive by the power forces they cannot overcome. Only by the intervention of a third party can bondage be broken and the person freed."[9]

Who, at one time or another, has not been victimized—who has never felt powerless? In particular, victims of physical and emotional abuse internalize the impact of feeling powerless. The adversary-kidnapper would want to lure you with his lie, "You are a powerless prisoner, a helpless hostage." But child of God, you are *not* powerless! The hostage-taker has no control over you. God has already redeemed you. Christ has already paid your ransom in full.

As Jesus proclaimed, "If the Son sets you free, you will be free indeed" (John 8:36). As you see yourself through God's eyes, you realize you've been redeemed in the most valuable ransom exchange in the history of the world—the Perfect Lamb bought your freedom.

Personalize these verses in your own words:

Matthew 20:28 _____

_____

_____

_____

_____

1 Corinthians 6:19-20 _____

_____

_____

_____

_____

Father, through Your eyes I can see that I... _____

_____

_____

_____

_____

I have confidence because...I am redeemed by God.

I Am Forgiven by God

"Blessed is he whose transgressions are forgiven"
(PSALM 32:1).

Have you ever felt the weight of choosing wrong...then the doubled weight of another's unforgiveness? Heaviness resides in the heart of the unforgiven.

Forgiveness is liberating—it lightens the loads of both the forgiven and the forgiver. One of the New Testament Greek words for *forgiveness* means to "loose away from, lift off, release." Imagine a cluster of helium balloons being released into the air, never to be seen again.

But a balloon cannot fly away when its string is tied to a heavy weight. Your sins create a heavy weight, one you cannot remove. When you trust Jesus Christ as your Savior, God cuts the string, removes the weight, and your sins fly away—you are forgiven! God forgives your sins through Christ's death. He releases the burden of wrong and sends it away.

It grieves us to realize every wrong word, every wrong act, and every wrong thought is marked down on a divine ledger sheet. God sees them all—even the things you thought no one else knew. He not only sees your actions, but He also knows your heart. Hebrews 4:13 says, "Nothing in all creation is hidden from God's sight. Everything is uncovered and laid bare before the eyes of him to whom we must give account."

Oh, the freedom of forgiveness when you, as a child of God, realize Jesus erased your ledger! This is why forgiveness is so totally liberating. As He hung dying on the cross, His blood was the payment for your wrong. Written across your ledger is *tetelestai* (Greek), which means "paid in full." Unlike human forgiveness, which is often forgiving but not forgetting, God has the capacity to instantly forgive you and remember your sins no more! Psalm 103:12 gives the assurance, "As far as the east is from the west, so far has he removed our transgressions from us."

As you see yourself through God's eyes, rejoice in your liberation! Your guilt is gone. Your sin will not be held against you—your heaviness is lifted, your heart is *released*. There truly is freedom in forgiveness.

Personalize these verses in your own words:

1 John 1:9 _____

_____

_____

_____

_____

Hebrews 8:12 _____

_____

_____

_____

_____

Father, through Your eyes I can see that I… _____

_____

_____

_____

_____

I have confidence because…I am forgiven by God.

I Am Washed by God

"Cleanse me with hyssop, and I will be clean;
wash me, and I will be whiter than snow"
(PSALM 51:7).

I remember a snowfall so clean and clear, so pure and perfectly white. The silent invitation to step into the new-fallen snow was irresistible. As I walked, I marveled at the soft snow blanketing the lawns and bushes. It was as though nature had been cleansed of all imperfections. On returning from my walk, however, I was saddened by the muddy tracks I had made. The ugly dirt underneath the pure snow had left its stain. No longer did the scene display a portrait so appealing.

The next morning, to my delight, God had quietly and lovingly covered the muddy track with a fresh new blanket of snow. There was no sign of the intruding walk I had taken the day before.

A fresh new day, a fresh new start.

Do you feel the landscape of your life is hopelessly marred by the muddy footprints of failure? Do you grieve with never-ending guilt because you stepped into sin and found yourself soiled and stained? "If only I could start over," you say, but you can't forgive yourself. Child of God, do you realize at the time of your salvation you were given both a fresh new heart and a fresh new start? You were cleansed and made whiter than snow.

Over a century ago, a hymn writer captured in melodious poetry the cleansing that took place in your heart when your sin was washed away:

> Lord Jesus, I long to be perfectly whole;
> I want Thee forever to live in my soul.
> Break down every idol, cast out ev'ry foe;

Now wash me and I shall be whiter than snow.
Whiter than snow, yes, whiter than snow;
Now wash me and I shall be whiter than snow.[10]

Because the Lord has cleansed you, you no longer carry the stain of sin. You have been covered by His blanket of holiness. Your sins are forgiven, never to be held against you. "'Come now, let us reason together,' says the LORD. 'Though your sins are like scarlet, they shall be as white as snow'" (Isaiah 1:18).

By seeing yourself through God's eyes, you can view each day as a fresh new day, a fresh new start!

Personalize these verses in your own words:

Psalm 51:10 _____

_____

_____

_____

_____

Ezekiel 36:25 _____

_____

_____

_____

_____

Father, through Your eyes I can see that I... _____

_____

_____

_____

_____

I have confidence because...I am washed whiter than snow.

Day 15

I Am Reconciled to God

"We were reconciled to him through the death of his Son"
(ROMANS 5:10).

Has your heart ever been broken over a shattered relationship? The closeness cut, a specialness severed? No matter how hard you tried, you couldn't restore harmony or unity. The pain of someone so dear taking on the form of an enemy was more than you could bear. You prayed for things to be different, for the clock to be turned back, for the opportunity to recapture what once had been.

Whether the broken relationship is between parent and child, husband and wife, or friend and friend, the heart has a longing to be reconciled. What a word of hope! The New Testament Greek word translated *reconciled* means "to change thoroughly, to exchange from one condition to another." *Reconciliation* means a personal relationship is changed—the heart of hostility is *exchanged* for a heart of harmony.

Sin destroys our harmonious relationship with God. It causes our hearts to be hostile toward Him. In reconciling us to Himself, the Father changes our "enemy" hearts so we can enjoy friendship with Him.

No other Bible story portrays God's heart of reconciliation more perfectly than that of the prodigal son, often called the most beautiful short story ever written. In Luke chapter 15, an ungrateful young son demands and receives his inheritance from his loving father. After quickly wasting his fortune, he awakens one day in the gutter. Friends and money gone, he finds a job feeding pigs—the most disgraceful job a Jewish boy could have! Finally, coming to his senses, he realizes his unworthiness and heads home, hoping only to be hired as a servant. But can he go home?

What a perfect setup for a father to say, "I told you so!" But not this father. Instead, upon seeing his wayward son in the distance, he is filled with compassion and runs to embrace the broken, repentant prodigal, exclaiming, "This son of mine was dead and is alive again" (Luke 15:24).

Do you realize your compassionate Father is waiting with open arms for your heart to be changed toward Him? What joy floods His heart the day you are reconciled to Him. Seeing yourself through God's eyes, you now enjoy warm friendship with God.

> I've wandered far away from God, now I'm coming home;
> The paths of sin too long I've trod, Lord, I'm coming home.
> Coming home, coming home, never more to roam,
> Open wide Thine arms of love, Lord, I'm coming home.[11]

Personalize these verses in your own words:

Romans 5:10 _____

_____

_____

_____

Colossians 1:22 _____

_____

_____

_____

Father, through Your eyes I can see that I... _____

_____

_____

_____

_____

I have confidence because...I am reconciled to God.

Part 3

My Possessions in Christ

*"He gives strength to the weary and increases
the power of the weak. Even youths grow tired
and weary, and young men stumble and fall;
but those who hope in the Lord will renew
their strength. They will soar on wings like eagles;
they will run and not grow weary,
they will walk and not be faint"*

(Isaiah 40:29-31).

I Am Given a New Heart by God

"I will give you a new heart and put a new spirit in you"
(EZEKIEL 36:26).

Many years ago, a friend brought me a clock from Switzerland. It was cleverly designed with a little bird that peeked out of its tiny house. But the clock wasn't very useful—it didn't keep the time correctly. It would "cuckoo" when it wasn't supposed to! Because I loved the clock, I took it to be repaired. The clocksmith examined the inside of my cherished gift and said it needed a new mainspring. Laughingly, he told me, "Your clock needs a new heart!"

This is true for more than clocks. Every *person* needs a new heart. Just look around you. How many parents have intentionally trained their children to lie, or encouraged them to steal from another child, or to yell at another, or to hit another? Very few, if any. Yet how many children have lied, stolen, yelled at, and hit others? All have. Why? Because their hearts have been self-seeking and self-centered from birth.

According to the Word of God, you were born with a sinful nature. Psalm 51:5 says, "Surely I was sinful at birth, sinful from the time my mother conceived me." And Jeremiah 17:9 adds, "The heart is deceitful above all things and beyond cure."

But the good news is that God said, "I will give you a new heart and put a new spirit in you." When you come into a genuine relationship with Christ, God puts a new heart inside you.

Your need is very similar to the need of someone who has a diseased heart and whose only hope for life is a heart transplant. In a spiritual sense, God takes your "diseased" heart and replaces it with a new one.

After this divine transplant, healing begins and, as promised, over time your new heart becomes capable of perfect love. Your self-centeredness is now Christ-centeredness. There is healing to replace the hatred, there is a balm for bitterness. You can face the world with a freedom and a future you have never known before.

"Create in me a pure heart, O God, and renew a steadfast spirit within me" (Psalm 51:10). Once you have a changed heart, you have a changed life. Seeing yourself through God's eyes, you can love the unlovable, be kind to the unkind, and forgive the unforgivable. All this because you have a new heart—God's heart.

Personalize these verses in your own words:

1 Timothy 1:5 _____

_____

_____

_____

_____

2 Timothy 2:22 _____

_____

_____

_____

_____

Father, through Your eyes I can see that I... _____

_____

_____

_____

_____

I have worth because...I am given a new heart by God.

I Am Given the Spirit of God

"We have...received...the Spirit who is from God"
(1 Corinthians 2:12).

An unexpected blackout took my neighborhood by surprise. One minute the lights were on, the next they were off. In total darkness, I inched my way to the bedside table and fumbled for the flashlight. Finding it, I flipped the switch. What frustration...the flashlight didn't work! How useless—a flashlight that didn't function.

Just as dysfunctional...just as unproductive...is the person who is not operating in the power of the Spirit. God has given each believer meaningful work to do, but it is to be done in *His strength*, by *His Spirit*. Many people rely totally on their own human abilities for power in their lives, whereas Zechariah 4:6 says it is "'not by might nor by power but by my Spirit,' says the Lord Almighty."

Likewise, many others simply don't know much about the Spirit of God, even though they are very familiar with Jesus and the heavenly Father. Yet the Bible has much to say about the role of the Holy Spirit. Specifically, "the Spirit helps us in our weakness" (Romans 8:26). What a blessing! And "the mind controlled by the Spirit is life and peace" (Romans 8:6). Think about it—those are huge benefits! Trying to serve God in our own strength is just as futile as trying to light our path with a dysfunctional flashlight.

Everyone knows the frustration of wandering in the dark. *Where do I go? What should I do? How am I to think?* When you are saved, you are also "marked in him with a seal, the promised Holy Spirit" (Ephesians 1:13). The Holy Spirit comes in to be the illuminator of your life and enlightens your path into the future.

Because He knows all—past, present, and future—He is the perfect guide for your life. "When he, the Spirit of truth, comes, he will guide you into all truth" (John 16:13). How? Your own personal counselor, conscience, and comforter fills your soul (mind, will, and emotions) with perfect truth. He teaches your mind, directs your will, and controls your emotions.

Like a flashlight, you were designed to shine, but you can never shine in your own power. The Holy Spirit, filling your human spirit, provides the power to produce the light. As you live dependent upon that power, you will shine as you were intended to…as a beautiful reflection of Christ Himself.

Realize, in God's eyes, you could never be useless when you have the privilege of such an intimate relationship with Him! "You are the light of the world" (Matthew 5:14).

Personalize these verses in your own words:

John 14:16 _____

_____

_____

_____

_____

1 Corinthians 6:19 _____

_____

_____

_____

_____

Father, through Your eyes I can see that I… _____

_____

_____

_____

_____

I have worth because…I am given the Holy Spirit.

Day 18

I Am Given Everything I Need by God

*"His divine power has given us everything
we need for life and godliness"*
(2 PETER 1:3).

Many years ago after opening my first bank account, I remember feeling really awkward. I was given a book of checks but didn't know how to use them! How embarrassing to have money in the bank and yet not know how to get it out.

I quickly learned, and not wanting my two younger sisters to experience this same confusion, I went to our neighborhood bank and opened checking accounts for each of them. I can still remember the exhilaration I felt as I made deposits in their names to accounts they hadn't even heard about, hadn't earned, and hadn't expected. Then I told them what I had done and taught them how to draw from their resources in the bank.

What heightened joy the heavenly Father must feel when He opens your personal account in His bank, the "Blessing Bank." Open 24 hours a day, this bank offers unlimited blessings and unlimited withdrawals.

Do you realize you actually have a spiritual bank account? The moment you become a child of God, He establishes your personal account with deposits vastly beyond your ability to exhaust. You are given every resource you will ever need to reflect the character of God within your life.

One major oversight committed by God's children is they don't open their bankbooks often enough to see the balance of their deposits. In reality, your bankbook, the Bible, discloses your personal assets in great detail. Are you troubled? Romans 5:1 shows your deposit of peace. Are you weak? Philippians 4:13 reveals your deposit of strength.

The entry in 2 Corinthians 5:5 indicates that God "has given us the Spirit as a deposit." And what a deposit...what a limitless reservoir of resources—God inside of us reproducing His life outside of us!

Do you feel angry? Do you need patience? Open your heart to the Spirit, and check the specific scriptures and promises He has deposited in your account to meet your needs. His presence accrues incredible interest. Galatians 5:22-23 declares the fruit of the Spirit yields "love, joy, peace, patience...and self-control," and is available for immediate withdrawal.

Are you spiritually bankrupt? Nothing would delight God more than for you to be "cashing your checks." Seeing yourself through God's eyes, you see His divine power has given you everything you need for life and godliness. You can bank on it!

Personalize these verses in your own words:

Ephesians 1:3 _____

_____

_____

_____

2 Corinthians 9:8 _____

_____

_____

_____

Father, through Your eyes I can see that I... _____

_____

_____

_____

_____

I have worth because...I am given everything I need by God.

I Am Given Strength from God

"The LORD gives strength to his people"
(PSALM 29:11).

For thousands of years a club has been in existence offering memberships throughout the world. It's a popular club, a prolific club. It's the "I Can't Club."

Under the bylaws, club members are required to make "I can't" statements with conviction: "I can't help but hate him after what he's done to me." "I can't quit this sin." "I can't forgive again!" Such fervor makes it sound as if each "I can't" statement is an unchangeable, universal law.

If you're a member, your pledge echoes the club's premise: No one can win over sin. You believe its promise: Defeat is normal. And you promote its purpose: to fill each mind with futility.

One law of science to which everyone is subject is the law of gravity—the force that pulls every object toward the center of the earth. Likewise, the members of the "I Can't Club" are prisoners to the downward pull of defeat. They are not only ground-bound, but also sin-bound.

Do you feel bound to a specific sin? Does quitting the "I Can't Club" seem impossible? As a child of God, the word *can't* doesn't have to control your life. Upon your salvation, He gives you the Spirit of God so that you will have the strength of God. He deals a deathblow to the "I Can't Club." He makes it possible for you to overcome any sin. How? By replacing one law for another: "The law of the Spirit of life set me free from the law of sin and death" (Romans 8:2).

Can you imagine a 190-ton mass of metal rising against the pull of gravity? Impossible! It can't be done! Oh, yes it can, by using a "higher law." When you, in faith, give yourself over to the principle of aerodynamics, you can enter an airplane with full confidence it will fly you from one city to another. You are no longer ground-bound.

Similarly, when you, in faith, give yourself over to the Spirit's control, the "I can't" statements will no longer keep you from leaving the runway of life. When God fills your spirit with His Spirit and infuses you with His strength, you no longer have to be sin-bound. Seeing yourself through God's eyes, you now know "I can" can cancel out "I can't" every time.

> *"He gives strength to the weary and increases the power of the weak ...But those who hope in the LORD will renew their strength. They will soar on wings like eagles"*
>
> (ISAIAH 40:29,31).

Personalize these verses in your own words:

Ephesians 3:16 _____

_____

_____

_____

_____

Philippians 4:13 _____

_____

_____

_____

_____

Father, through Your eyes I can see that I... _____

_____

_____

_____

_____

I have worth because...I am given strength from God.

Day 20

I Am Given the Mercy of God

"I will have mercy on whom I will have mercy"
(Exodus 33:19).

All eyes are on the woman. Her face is masked with fear. Heart pounding and blood racing, her mind is frantic as the Pharisees fling her before Christ and the curious crowd. Her fate lies with them. With slanderous delight, her accusers recount how she had been caught in the act of adultery. Reminding Jesus that according to Jewish law she must be stoned, they demand, "Now what do you say?" (John 8:5).

As Jesus' eyes scan the crowd He realizes an opportune time has come to teach a lesson about compassion, as well as conviction of sin. And Jesus' concern is for this woman's soul rather than for her sin. He shifts the focus to the "faultless" Pharisees, stating, "He that is without sin among you, let him first cast a stone at her" (John 8:7 KJV). What? You mean they must scrutinize *themselves?* The Lord cut open the conscience of the crowd. One by one they retreat, dropping their stones and leaving the woman alone to face the Man of mercy, the only One who could rightfully throw a stone.

"Has no one condemned you?" asks Jesus. "Neither do I condemn you...go now and leave your life of sin" (verse 11). Jesus looked past her fault, saw her need, forgave her sin, set her free. An adulteress deserving death is given another chance at life. What matchless mercy!

Mercy means, literally, "the outward manifestation of pity." Mercy is more than emotion; it is *active compassion* meeting a need. No one has a right to mercy. It is extended simply because of the heart of the giver and the need of the receiver. Therefore, when God extends His mercy, He naturally expresses His heart of compassion.

God has given you, His child, an invaluable coin of compassion. One side is engraved with grace, the other is minted with mercy.

Throughout your life He extends both grace (*giving* you what you *do not* deserve—liberation) and mercy (*not giving* you what you *do* deserve—condemnation).

You can't buy the coin—it's priceless. You can't earn the coin—it's undeserved. In fact, you can't merit mercy. If you could, it wouldn't be mercy.

Child of God, seeing yourself through God's eyes, you can know you are forgiven—not by merit, but by mercy. What compassion from the Man of mercy!

Personalize these verses in your own words:

Isaiah 55:7 _____

_____

_____

_____

_____

Hebrews 4:16 _____

_____

_____

_____

_____

Father, through Your eyes I can see that I... _____

_____

_____

_____

_____

I have worth because...I am given the mercy of God.

I Am Given the Grace of God

"He gives us more grace"
(JAMES 4:6).

My all-time favorite class was ninth-grade algebra. I loved puzzles, which made algebra fun. Because subjects were hard for me, my A's in algebra helped to soothe my suffering self-image. In math class, I faced each test with confidence! Tuesday's test would be no different.

But while taking the test, I suddenly found that I couldn't remember the formula for problem number one…and number two…or three, four, and five…my mind had gone blank! I could solve only the last two problems. Stunned, I handed my paper to the teacher. After a long, pensive pause, she asked, "When do you have study hall tomorrow?" "At ten o'clock," I nervously replied. The next day at ten sharp I was in my algebra classroom, and I was given a second chance. I was given a gift called *grace*.

Before even knowing what the word *grace* meant, I knew what it was like to be impacted by it. I was awed a teacher would extend undeserved favor toward me. That's what the New Testament Greek word for *grace* means: "undeserved care, unearned favor."

God is a God of second chances. He is a God full of grace, a God who not only saves you from eternal death, but also saves you from a defeated life. He saves you by putting His life in you. If you focus only on what it's like to fail in certain areas of your life, you could be drawn into the downward spiral of dejection. However, Jesus said, "I have come that they might have life, and have it to the full" (John 10:10).

> He giveth more grace when the burden grows greater;
> He sendeth more strength when the labors increase.
> To added affliction He addeth His mercy;

To multiplied trials, His multiplied peace.
His love has no limit; His grace has no measure;
His pow'r has no boundary known unto men.
For out of His infinite riches in Jesus,
He giveth, and giveth, and giveth again![12]

Can you really have fullness when you have failed? Oh, child of God, discouragement, defeat, and dejection are what the God of all grace can save you from! Seeing yourself through God's eyes, you will find that in your weakness, He will be your strength. In your failure, He will give you fullness.

How blessed you are to know the God of grace, who saves you from your failures. He is the God of the second chance...and the third... and the fourth...and the fifth...

Personalize these verses in your own words:

2 Corinthians 12:9 _____
_____
_____
_____

1 Timothy 1:14 _____
_____
_____
_____

Father, through Your eyes I can see that I... _____
_____
_____
_____
_____

I have worth because... I am given the grace of God.

I Am Given Complete Access to God

"In him and through faith in him we may approach
God with freedom and confidence"
(EPHESIANS 3:12).

As you were growing up, what kind of "signs" did your father wear? Was he labeled *approachable...available...accessible?* I'll never forget my best friend's father. He wore those signs naturally and never once threatened to remove them. As a teenager, I was continually drawn to him and always felt valuable in his presence while in their home.

The life of this man, so accessible, was in sharp contrast to the life of my father, who enforced his belief that children should be seen and not heard. I was so intimidated by his austerity that occasionally, upon hearing his footsteps, I would hide behind a door. It was never normal for me to sit in his lap, kiss his cheek, or share my secrets. I felt my father wore signs that blared, KEEP OUT...NO TRESPASSING... DO NOT ENTER!

Each evening after dinner, my father demanded the full attention of my mother, literally forbidding her to be with us. I will always remember the loneliness of being barred from receiving my mother's care and concern night after night.

Many people think of God in the same way as I perceived my father—imposing, powerful, completely inaccessible, and certainly not interested in the details of their lives.

But is that true of God? Do you know what your heavenly Father is really like? In John 14:8, Philip emphatically said, "Show us the Father." Jesus responded, "Anyone who has seen me has seen the Father...I am in the Father, and...the Father is in me" (John 14:9-10). The truth about God can be found in Jesus.

Being accessible to the poor, Jesus did not wear fashion labels for the elite. He wore no *unapproachable* labels for the leper. Even the prostitute was moved by His openness. And when the children tried to get close to Him, Jesus rebuked His disciples for trying to pin on Him the label *unavailable.* From child to leper, from seeker to sinner, no one felt unacceptable in the presence of Jesus. Though He is Almighty God in the flesh, He is always accessible. From the beginning of time to today, God is always accessible to you!

Whether or not you have ever experienced access to a loving, earthly father, you are always welcome into the presence of your heavenly Father. Seeing yourself through God's eyes, you know He never has a DO NOT ENTER sign over His heart.

Personalize these verses in your own words:

Ephesians 2:18 _____

_____

_____

_____

Hebrews 4:16 _____

_____

_____

_____

Father, through Your eyes I can see that I… _____

_____

_____

_____

I have worth because…I am given access to God.

I Am Given the Mind of Christ

"We have the mind of Christ"
(1 Corinthians 2:16).

One cold evening, the fire was warming, as was our conversation. I was spending special time with one of my closest friends—one whom I've known for many years. Several times during the evening, I would start to say something and before I could get my thoughts completely formed, she would finish my sentence. Twice, I remember, we said the same word at the same time.

My friend and I have a unique oneness of mind and spirit. We know each other's sensitivities and sorrows, the preferences and the pains.

How amazing it is that God offers you the same oneness with His Son. He wants you to know His heart by knowing His Word. He wants His thinking to saturate your thoughts. His plan from the beginning has been that His nature become your "second nature."

When you are given a new life in Christ, you are given a new nature. *Nature* simply means doing what comes naturally. God gives you the capacity to think as He naturally thinks. What an extraordinary gift!

A writer friend of mine told me every time she sits down to write, she first prays she will have the mind of Christ—His thoughts flowing through her as she writes. Her comment had a strong impact on me—I now pray in the same way.

In the midst of confusion, you need the mind of Christ. In the midst of conflict, when criticism is caustic and when advice is adversarial, you need the mind of Christ. As long as you live, there will always be those who are mentally and emotionally on the attack.

Remember Job's "friends"? Although Job had done nothing wrong, he was besieged with assumptions that he had sinned. He was weighed down by their words, and volumes of verbiage.

At times you may feel like Job, wondering what is true. The advice-givers go on and on, weaving their webs of words. Somehow you feel caught. Can you possibly break free? The answer is yes, because as you develop the mind of Christ, His divine wisdom and discernment are available to you as well.

Knowing the mind of Christ comes from times spent with Him and His Word. Seeing yourself through God's eyes, you develop a deeper oneness of mind and spirit. There can be no greater basis for friendship!

Personalize these verses in your own words:

Romans 12:1-2 _____

_____

_____

_____

Ephesians 4:23 _____

_____

_____

_____

Father, through Your eyes I can see that I... _____

_____

_____

_____

_____

I have worth because...I am given the mind of Christ.

Part 4

God's Purpose for Me

*"His divine power has given us everything we need
for life and godliness through our knowledge of him
who called us by his own glory and goodness"*

(2 Peter 1:3).

Day 24

I Am Created to Do Good Works for Christ

"We are...created in Christ Jesus to do good works,
which God prepared in advance for us to do"
(EPHESIANS 2:10).

We all know what it is like to feel small. As we look around us, it is easy to see people who are performing with peak proficiency, people who are being accomplished with quickness and creativity. In comparison, we often feel small and feel that we are inadequate, incapable, even inept.

But here's something important to remember: In God's economy, bigger isn't always better. Remember the poor widow in Luke chapter 21 who gave her gift to God? Her "widow's mite" was the equivalent of only one-twentieth of a penny. Based not on the size of her gift, but on the size of her sacrifice, Jesus singled her out, saying, "This poor widow has put in more than all the others" (Luke 21:3). He was indicating the small offering from her humble heart had far more value than all the other gifts. The widow's mite was mighty—she had given with a sacrificial heart.

The issue is not size, but sacrifice. The smallest kindness, the smallest deed, will not go unnoticed by God. A small work is a great work when the heart motive is right in God's sight.

A.W. Tozer wrote, "It is not what a man does that determines whether his work is sacred or secular, it is why he does it. The motive is everything. Let a man sanctify the Lord God in his heart and he can thereafter do no common act."[13]

As a child of God, do you realize God has already prepared, in advance, a fulfilling and meaningful work for you to do? This plan was in His mind even before you became His child. Perhaps you might think, *But I'm not really capable of doing anything significant.* Be assured right now you are fully equipped to do a precious work, a powerful work, a work of love.

I know a woman who takes the "teddy bear stance." All teddy bears have one common characteristic: their arms are open wide. Think of the people in our world who are never hugged. What a ministry this dear woman has—encouraging others with a warm embrace! She stands with her arms open wide, ready to share God's love.

Have you ever felt insignificant because no one noticed you were reaching out? Your sacrificial effort may have seemed too small to be appreciated. Remember, as you see yourself through God's eyes, you can know even an unseen deed is not hidden from His view: "Whatever you did for one of the least of these…you did for me" (Matthew 25:40). In God's sight, no sacrifice of the heart is small.

Personalize these verses in your own words:

Psalm 90:17 _____
_____
_____
_____

Colossians 3:23 _____
_____
_____
_____

Father, through Your eyes I can see that I… _____
_____
_____
_____
_____

I have value because…I am created to do good works for Christ.

I Am an Ambassador for Christ

"We are...Christ's ambassadors"
(2 CORINTHIANS 5:20).

The little girl with blond curls tapped across the screen into the hearts of millions. Her charm attracted children around the world. Dolls with her name flooded the market. The Texas Rangers eventually made her a captain, while the state of Kentucky made her a colonel. The 165,000-member Kiddies Club of England vowed to "follow faithfully the example she set in character, behavior and personal manners." The phenomenon grew as she starred in film after film.

A reporter once asked, "Shirley Temple, don't you ever get tired of people pushing and shoving, asking questions and demanding your time?" "No, I don't mind at all," she said. "It's part of my job." This was a little girl setting an example, a little girl living to the highest potential of her calling.

Child of God, you too have a calling. Ephesians 4:1 says, "Live a life worthy of the calling you have received." What is your calling? To be an ambassador!

In 1974, U.S. President Gerald Ford appointed Shirley Temple Black as an ambassador to officially represent the United States to the people of Ghana. What a position of trust! An ambassador is an official messenger of the highest rank sent by one government to another. This resident representative holds sovereign authority from the homeland to represent, speak, minister, influence, and negotiate. You too have been called to be an ambassador—you are a representative of Christ to a spiritually starved world in need of the Master's message.

Perhaps you're thinking, *Others might qualify as an ambassador, but not me! I don't have the freedom or the language to be an ambassador—especially in my family or workplace.* Realize God's power to speak through you has no constraint. The apostle Paul understood this when he said, while in prison, "Pray also for me, that whenever I open my mouth, words may be given me so that I will fearlessly make known the mystery of the gospel, for which I am an ambassador in chains" (Ephesians 6:19-20).

Because Christ lives in you, His character will be lived through you. You will minister with His mercy. You will represent His righteousness. You will speak with His strength. Even when you don't have the freedom to speak, remember your influence will be conveyed through His Spirit.

Seeing yourself through God's eyes, you are an appointed ambassador, called by the King!

Personalize these verses in your own words:

Ephesians 4:1 _____

_____

_____

_____

Matthew 5:14-16 _____

_____

_____

_____

Father, through Your eyes I can see that I… _____

_____

_____

_____

I have value because…I am an ambassador for Christ.

I Am Being Conformed to Christ

*"Those God foreknew he also predestined
to be conformed to the likeness of his Son"*
(ROMANS 8:29).

Before a thrilled Olympic audience in 1976, Dorothy Hamill created a sensation as she skated to victory with her "Hamill camel." Yet even more amazing was the fashion sensation she created with a haircut known as "the wedge," later called the "Hamill haircut." In a matter of days, large numbers of Dorothy Hamill look-alikes took to the ice trying to be duplicates of Dorothy.

Have you ever tried to look like someone else? You bought designer clothes, but they only covered your insecurities. You changed your hairstyle, but that didn't change your self-doubt. How you tried to conform to that which was popular!

The word *conformed* can refer to something transitory and changeable, much like Dorothy's hairstyle—in one year and out the next. However, when God says He predestined you "to be conformed" to Christ, He is not referring to a transitory *outer* change, but to a transforming *inner* change. When you are conformed to Christlikeness, you are given the ability to have His character on the inside. This will change your conduct on the outside. You will not be pulled by the popular, pushed by the press, or overpowered by politics. Just as Jesus was not shaped and molded by what was happening around Him, you too can withstand external pressure and influences by allowing the character of Christ to develop within you.

One man whose character was conformed to Christ's was Olympian Eric Liddell. In the 1924 Olympics in Paris, this Scotsman was Great Britain's hope for winning the 100-meter race. Then came the shocking announcement: The qualifying heat was to be run on a Sunday.

Unthinkable! Eric believed the Sabbath was God's day. He resolved, "I'm not running the 100-meter race"—not for Scotland, not for Britain, not even for the gold. Though labeled a traitor, he refused to conform to rules that went against his conscience. Instead, Eric began to train for the 400-meter race.

On the day of the race, Eric approached the starting blocks with determination. His qualifying times had not been spectacular, and his contenders were excellent runners. The gun sounded. He was off like a bullet. Flying through the wind, Eric crossed the finish line and set a new world record, winning five full meters ahead of his nearest competitor. From international jeers to cheers, he has been admired for decades as the one who would not conform to the pressures of this world. Why? Because his very life was conformed to the character of Christ. Seeing yourself through God's eyes, you are being conformed to the image of God's plan for your life. You will be amazed with His results!

Personalize these verses in your own words:

Hebrews 12:1 _____

_____

_____

_____

Romans 12:2 _____

_____

_____

_____

Father, through Your eyes I can see that I... _____

_____

_____

_____

I have value because...I am being conformed to Christ.

Day 27

I Am Complete in Christ

"You have been made complete"
(COLOSSIANS 2:10 NASB).

Interernational fame came in 1919 when his calculations bedazzled the world. He was considered the greatest genius on earth. His theories of relativity revolutionized the scientific community. Highly sought after, he traveled to speak in capitals all over the world. He admitted, however, "It is strange to be known so universally and yet to be so lonely."

These words of Albert Einstein mirror the pain and pathos that have oppressed many human hearts. Loneliness presents a paradox: How can such heaviness come from emptiness? The answer lies in the fact the heart yearns to be connected with someone significant. God made us this way. However, we have all experienced loneliness, which is the state of being cut off from others, or a lack of connectedness with others.

The greatest fear of most single people is loneliness. In 1950, one out of every ten households was a single-person household (9.5 percent). But in 2000, the number of single-person households jumped to one in four (26 percent).[14] Sadly, singles often live under the black cloud of incompleteness. Emotional rain clouds, molded by well-meaning friends, pour out their promises: "One day Mr. Right will come and complete you!" "One day you'll find someone who will make you whole." No wonder the single is fearful—who wants to be half a person?

Child of God, at the moment of your salvation you receive the indwelling Christ, whose presence produces total fulfillment, complete wholeness. Colossians 2:9-10 gives the assurance, "In Christ all the fullness of the Deity lives in bodily form, and you have been given fullness in Christ." To be full is to be complete at the highest or greatest degree. It is the Savior, not a spouse, who completes you.

Three myths need to be blown away: (1) Singles are always lonely people. No! But they can experience times of isolation. (2) Singles are not whole people. No! When you have Christ in you, you have the fullness of His deity in you to live through you. (3) Only singles are lonely. No! Married individuals can also experience loneliness. But as you see yourself through God's eyes, whether married or single, you can blow away those black clouds of incompleteness and say with confidence, "I am one complete person, and one is a *whole* number!"

Personalize these verses in your own words:

John 17:22-23 _____

_____

_____

_____

_____

2 Peter 1:3-4 _____

_____

_____

_____

_____

Father, through Your eyes I can see that I... _____

_____

_____

_____

_____

I have value because...I am complete in Christ.

I Am Clothed with the Righteousness of Christ

"I put on righteousness as my clothing"
(JOB 29:14).

You're at the beach...you're famished...you find a restaurant...you rush in...you spot a sign: "No shirt, no shoes, no service." The message is clear. To be accepted, you must be clothed according to the restaurant's standard.

God also has a standard. But He makes it possible for you to be acceptable to Him at all times when He gives you "righteousness as [your] clothing." The word *righteous,* in its simplest form, means "right" and "just." The word also means "acquitted, vindicated." Your faith and trust in Christ enables God to acquit you of sin. He doesn't see your sin any longer, but sees you as clothed with the righteousness of Christ. As such, you are acceptable and properly dressed to "come and dine, and have fellowship with God any time you desire."

More specifically, *righteousness* has two similar yet distinct meanings:

- First, being right in God's sight—based on belief.
- Second, doing right in God's sight—based on behavior.

The problem with the second meaning is this: "There is no one righteous, not even one" (Romans 3:10). Therefore, if you wanted God's acceptance, it couldn't be based on all your actions being right in His sight. God knew you needed to *be* right so you could learn to *do* right.

If you have struggled with feeling too unworthy to be called "the righteousness of God" (2 Corinthians 5:21), realize this clothing God has given you is like a uniform of authority.

Have you ever seen a gigantic 18-wheeler grinding to a stop just because a police officer walks in front of the traffic and holds up a hand? What gives this person the right to command such respect? Certainly not parentage, social status, education, personality, or even church affiliation. The officer stands confidently in front of this awesome "king of the road" because of the right clothing—the uniform signifies authority.

Did you realize at the moment of your conversion, you were issued a righteous "uniform"? All of your sins, past, present, and future, were forgiven, and you were given power and authority over sin. With the "breastplate of righteousness" (Ephesians 6:14), you no longer have to give in to sin; it is no longer "master" over you.

As you see yourself through God's eyes, as His child, you have power that backs the "badge." That's how God sees you!

Personalize these verses in your own words:

2 Corinthians 5:21 _____

_____

_____

_____

Galatians 3:27 _____

_____

_____

_____

Father, through Your eyes I can see that I... _____

_____

_____

_____

I have value because...I am clothed with the righteousness of God.

I Am Holy Before God

"God did not call us to be impure, but to live a holy life"
(1 Thessalonians 4:7).

Have you ever had difficulty with the Scripture passage, "Be holy, because I am holy" (1 Peter 1:16)? Because most people think being holy is synonymous with being sinless, they think, *Who could possibly be holy? It's unattainable…unimaginable!*

One day a friend said to me, "I know *holy* means 'set apart,' but I don't want to be set apart. That sounds like having a constant case of measles!" Unfortunately, some people consider a holy person as one who lives a monklike existence, praying 24 hours a day so as not to sin. Holiness, however, does not bring about isolation, but integration—the integration of the character of Christ in you for His nature to be expressed *through* you. *Nature* simply means "that which is natural."

When I was a little girl, my Uncle Jimmy walked me through his watermelon patch in Idabel, Oklahoma. Holding up a tiny black seed, he said, "These big melons grew from seeds just like this one." That seemed impossible to me! Yet 80 miles from Idabel is the town of Hope, Arkansas, where something "more impossible" became reality. Lloyd Bright gave his watermelon seed the care and environment to grow naturally. The result? A world-record 268.8-pound watermelon![15] How? Watermelon seeds simply do what comes naturally to them—they grow. Their seeds are *set apart* by God for that purpose.

When you are set apart by God, holiness is natural. The Father is the gardener; Christ is the seed. With Christ in you, you are set apart to grow and become like Him. First John 3:9 explains: "No one who is born of God will continue to sin, because God's seed remains in him." It is natural for the Lord not to sin. Therefore, with God's seed in you, it becomes increasingly natural for you not to sin. What seems impossible becomes possible. You are set apart *from sin* and set apart *to God*. You will not become instantly sinless, but you will sin less... and less...and less.

As you see yourself through God's eyes and with His presence inside you, He will produce the impossible through you. Why settle for anything less?

Personalize these verses in your own words:

Romans 12:1 _____

_____

_____

_____

_____

2 Corinthians 7:1 _____

_____

_____

_____

_____

Father, through Your eyes I can see that I... _____

_____

_____

_____

_____

I have value because...I am holy before God.

I Am Safe in the Protection of God

"You alone, O Lord,
make me dwell in safety"
(Psalm 4:8).

Tammy, the young trapeze artist, electrified the audience with her daring performance. Afterward, a reporter asked, "How do you appear so confident performing such a dangerous aerial act?" The child quickly broke into a smile and responded, "That's easy. Didn't you see the safety net? There was a man standing there to break my fall. That was my dad."

Nothing frees you to walk the tightrope of life—to perform daring feats outside your comfort zone—like knowing you're safe in your heavenly Father's care. He holds the net. In Deuteronomy 33:27 we are promised, "Underneath are the everlasting arms," always ready to break our fall.

As a child of God, you face seemingly insurmountable challenges—trying times when God forges your faith under pressure. During these times of severe stress, you can quell your fears by remembering...*He holds the net.* Then your circumstances get a little shaky and you are wobbling back and forth between faith and fear, even if you slip off the tightrope of life and take a dive, your Father will break the fall... because He holds firmly on the net.

In the midst of a storm, when Simon Peter saw Jesus walking on the water, he yearned to step toward the safety of Jesus. In a burst of faith he cried out, "Jesus, let me come to You!" Throwing caution to the wind, he stepped out onto the water toward Jesus. When Peter became frightened, he began to sink but only momentarily, for Jesus was there to help him.

Later, however, Peter experienced a devastating fall: He denied his

Lord—not once, not twice, but three times. He had been trusted, but now he was a failure.

Yet Peter fell into Jesus' unbreakable net of safety, acceptance, and love. Jesus was there with a net full of forgiveness for Peter. Jesus broke the fall.

Where there had been a threefold denial, now Jesus gave Peter the opportunity for a threefold declaration of love: Peter, do you love Me? Tend My lambs...shepherd My sheep...feed My sheep (see John 21:15-17). The Lord's gentle coaching prepared Peter for a lifetime of confident ministry.

Do you know the sickening feeling of plummeting toward failure? See yourself through God's eyes, and never forget that He stands to break your fall. He ensures your safety; *He holds the net.*

Personalize these verses in your own words:

Psalm 16:1 _____

_____

_____

Romans 8:31 _____

_____

_____

Father, through Your eyes I can see that I... _____

_____

_____

_____

I have value because...I am safe in the protection of God.

I Am Secure in the Love of God

"I have loved you with an everlasting love"
(JEREMIAH 31:3).

Who has not longed for love? Who has not sought security, devotion, and commitment from one significant person, only to find himself empty-handed and empty-hearted? God created each person with an inner need for unconditional love. Yet we all know what it is like to have loved and lost.

This is why the love of God is unfathomable. As a child of God, you can never be lost from His love. Nothing you can do will make God love you more. Nothing you can do will make God love you less. He loves you without merit; He loves you without measure.

From 1857 to 1866, when attempts were made to lay a transatlantic telegraph cable between Europe and North America, workmen discovered ocean depths they were unable to fathom, depths they were unable to measure or to probe. A weighted line dropped to a depth of 2,000 fathoms (one fathom equals six feet) still did not reach the ocean floor. This depth was called "unfathomable." Similarly, the depth of God's love is beyond measure. "Can you fathom the mysteries of God? Can you probe the limits of the Almighty?" (Job 11:7). Imagine, if you can, this is God's love for you!

Perhaps the most poetic expression of God's unfathomable love was written long ago by a man who died in an asylum. These words were found scribbled on the wall beside his bed:

> Could we with ink the ocean fill,
> And were the skies of parchment made;
> Were ev'ry stalk on earth a quill,
> And ev'ry man a scribe by trade;

To write the love of God above
Would drain the ocean dry;
Nor could the scroll contain the whole,
Though stretched from sky to sky.

Later, Frederick Lehman added these words in penning the song
The Love of God:

O love of God, how rich and pure!
How measureless and strong!
It shall forevermore endure—
The saints' and angels' song.[16]

How, then, can you even begin to grasp the love of God? In part, by looking at Christ's sacrificial death on the cross, and His resurrection, and His love for you. His death redeems you; His sacrifice saves you; His life liberates you. In love, He laid down His life for you so His life could be lived through you.

Seeing yourself through God's eyes, you can be assured His love never fails—it is forgiving, freeing...fathomless.

Personalize these verses in your own words:

Ephesians 3:17-19 _____

_____

_____

Romans 8:38-39 _____

_____

_____

Father, through Your eyes I can see that I... _____

_____

_____

I have value...because I am secure in the love of God.

Part 5

LEADER'S GUIDE

Leading a Study Group

Thank you for making a commitment to lead your fellow believers in a study of *Seeing Yourself Through God's Eyes*. It takes a special kind of courage and devotion to open your heart to others, and to create a safe and sacred place where the Christian life can be nourished so it will blossom, grow, and bear fruit. As a leader, you are a laborer in the most important work there is: helping the family of Christ become Christlike—one precious soul at a time.

All of God's children have a vital need to understand their true identity—all of us need to know who we are "in Christ." This reality was the driving force behind my decision to write *Seeing Yourself Through God's Eyes*. As the apostle Paul wrote, "If anyone is in Christ, he is a new creation; the old has gone, the new has come!" (2 Corinthians 5:17). To help Christians see what it really means to be a "new creation"—chosen, loved, and accepted unconditionally by God—is an invaluable and life-changing ministry.

Of course, this doesn't mean the task is always easy. It can feel intimidating to face a room full of people—some expectant and eager, others perhaps reserved and reluctant—all looking to you for wisdom and guidance. Along the way you may be tempted to ask yourself, *Why did I ever agree to lead a Bible study on this 31-day devotional?* That's why I've included a group leader's guide, which provides you with practical suggestions and discussion questions. Use them—and free yourself to remember why you volunteered to lead in the first place:

- Because you are hungry for a walk with God that works "where the rubber meets the road"—in the heat and friction of everyday life.

- Because you desire the fellowship of other believers who will walk alongside you.

- Because deep down you know a leader is really only a fellow traveler on this spiritual journey, a humble seeker like everyone else.

Most of all, remember this: You are not alone—far from it. Simply trust the One who lives within you. Ask for *His* wisdom, and you will find the knowledge and spiritual growth you and others are seeking.

Before the First Meeting

Pray. Ask God to bring into your group the people of His choosing.

Determine the size of your group. Seeing Yourself Through God's Eyes is appropriate for home Bible study groups, counseling and support groups, as well as for church and business groups. The optimal size of a group is 8 to 12 members. When a group has more than 12 members, it may be best to divide into two groups. People tend to share more freely and to develop greater intimacy in smaller groups.

Know the structure of the study. Seeing Yourself Through God's Eyes is a four-week study featuring 31 daily lessons, with each lesson taking about 10 to 15 minutes to complete. You may want to schedule an introductory session in order to give an overview of the study. (Use pages 17-18 of the book as an example.) The recommended length of time for group discussion is approximately 45 to 60 minutes.

Schedule the dates and times. Contact group members far enough in advance so they can plan ahead to attend.

- Send out a reminder card or e-mail a few days prior to the first meeting.

- Include dates and times the study group will meet, address and contact information, anticipated preparation time per week, and length of group discussion time allotted each week.

State expectations. Give the following details:

- When members will receive their books and the cost of the book, if not prepaid.

- What, if anything, members should do prior to the first meeting.

- Supplies they will need to bring each week (a Bible, the book, notebook paper, and pen).

- Regular attendance and sharing.

Get name tags. Attempt to learn everyone's name beforehand so you can introduce them to each other at the first meeting.

Strategies for Successfully Leading a Small Group

Pray for the members of your group throughout the week. Acknowledge your dependence on the Holy Spirit, and trust Him to penetrate every person's heart with biblical truths.

Start and stop on time. Be respectful of the group members' time.

Welcome each person. Learn to address everyone by name.

Use "icebreakers" to get better acquainted. You may want to begin the first meeting with questions such as, "Why did you decide to join this group?" and "What do you hope to gain from this study?" Also, you may want to ask everyone to introduce themselves and tell something about their background or family.

Explain the question-and-answer format. Reassure members they are not expected to share anything that makes them feel uncomfortable. Make the main focus God's Word. Since each daily reading concludes with three exercises, you may use some of these to stimulate discussion. Suggested questions are also provided in the following pages. Use them to help guide your discussion, but don't feel confined by them—follow the Holy Spirit's leading and adapt the study to best meet the needs of your group.

Be a facilitator, not a teacher. A teacher presents his or her own information in a clear, understandable way to others. A facilitator leads the group members to discuss what they have learned during the week. By asking thought-provoking questions and creating a reassuring environment, a facilitator helps the group members discover ways to personally apply the truths revealed in God's Word.

Pace the meeting to cover the lesson in the allotted time. It may be helpful to write, in the margin of your workbook, the time you expect to reach the halfway point in the discussion. Pencil in other times, allowing about six to eight minutes for each question (some will be covered more quickly than others).

Encourage interaction. Most of the questions provided in this guide are structured to allow for a variety of responses. Encourage members to share their own insights and experiences.

Take a literal approach to Scripture unless the passage is clearly figurative. The Bible means what it says. While there is only one correct interpretation of a particular passage, there are many applications. Don't argue over interpretations or obscure meanings. Give group members the freedom to express their views without fear of criticism or embarrassment.

Respect members' answers. Even if you disagree with someone's comments or have a different perspective, resist the urge to prove your point or "win the argument." Show your respect by saying, "I appreciate your thoughts about this," Or, "I can tell you have been thinking about this subject." If someone presents an opinion that is controversial, you might say, "I've never thought of it that way." Or, "Does anyone else have another opinion?"

Remember you are not responsible for the spiritual growth of another person. Spiritual growth takes place as the Spirit of God works in the life of each person. It does not occur at the same rate for everyone.

Discuss questionable comments in private. If someone makes a judgmental, unwholesome, or off-the-wall comment, steer the person and the group back on track by saying, "That's a concept I'd like to discuss with you at another time," or "Let's finish today's study and then maybe you and I can discuss this afterward." (If you say you will discuss it later, be sure to follow up.)

Try to include everybody in the discussion. Some people are shy and reluctant to speak out in a group. Others may have problems they cannot openly reveal. Be sensitive to their unspoken needs and to those who are introverted.

Gently keep long-winded people from dominating. While some people are reticent to speak out, others have the opposite problem— they talk too much. Offer a noncondemning statement such as: "You raise some good points. Does anyone else want to respond?" Or, "I wonder if someone else wants to share an opinion."

Learn to be comfortable saying, "I don't know." Just because you're the leader doesn't mean you have to know everything. It's fine to say, "I don't know the answer, but I will find out before our next meeting." (Hope for the Heart has written *Biblical Counseling Keys* addressing such topics as identity, self-worth, and purpose in life, as well as over 100 other resources that can be obtained through the website at www.hopefortheheart.org.)

Understand that silence is okay. When you ask a question, give the group members time to think. Wait quietly for several seconds so people can consider how they might respond.

Rephrase the question if there is no response. You might say, "Let me put it another way…" Occasionally, you may want to drop the question entirely and move on to the next question.

Share your answers last. Your answers to the discussion questions should be considered as equal in importance to the answers of any other member of the group. Usually it is best to give your opinion *after* the other group members have had a chance to express their thoughts.

Close the meeting with prayer. If you're nearing the agreed-upon ending time, ask if someone would like to close the study with prayer (or do so yourself). If time allows, you may choose to take prayer requests.

It's possible that, during the course of your study, you will observe certain participants who would make effective group leaders themselves. Consider encouraging them to seek the Lord's guidance about leading their own *Seeing Yourself Through God's Eyes* study with another person or group—taking what they have learned and sharing it with others, in the spirit of Proverbs 27:17.

Days 1-7
My Position in Christ

"Find rest, O my soul, in God alone;
my hope comes from him.
He alone is my rock and my salvation;
he is my fortress, I will not be shaken"

(PSALM 62:5-6).

Back in the days when courageous explorers traveled the oceans in sailing ships, they paid a lot of money for maps accurately depicting the geography of the known world. It was of utmost importance to know precisely where they were at all times. This wasn't just a matter of navigating successfully to their destination. They believed a mariner who lost sight of familiar landmarks risked wandering off the edges of the map, into unknown waters teeming with terrifying sea monsters. If they strayed too far, whole ships and entire crews could fall off the rim of the world, never to be seen again.

Of course, today we are amused by such backward thinking and unfounded fears. Cartographers (mapmakers) have mapped the whole globe and know better.

Yet many of us, as believers, are very much like those superstitious sailors. Without knowing our precise *position* within God's kingdom, we mistakenly believe there might be unknown regions where His grace no longer applies to us or treacherous currents that might plunge us into peril. Under these conditions, fear keeps us from trusting the One who would lead us away from the shores of our old existence toward a new life of freedom and grace.

Knowing *who you are* "in Christ" begins by learning *where you stand*. Here's the truth of the matter: As one who has cried out to God for salvation, you are always sheltered under His protective sovereignty. You are never beyond His tender love and saving grace. There are no edges to the territory of His kingdom. To be a believer is to forever occupy a position of forgiveness and favor with your Creator—the God of all there is—no matter where you are.

There is no safer place than that.

Day 1: I Am Adopted by God

- Regardless of your family ties, you can draw comfort from knowing you have been adopted into God's family. What are some of the similarities and differences between the legal adoption of a child into a family and the spiritual adoption of a person into God's family?

- Read Galatians 4:5-7 out loud. What benefits and blessings do believers receive when adopted into God's family?

Day 2: I Am a Child of God

- Every person has an inward "longing to belong." God Himself put this feeling into our hearts. Why do you think God put this longing in us? How does this longing reveal itself in your life?

- According to John 1:12, how does a person become a true child of God?

Day 3: I Am Precious to God

- When we face difficulties in life, we might be tempted to doubt that we are truly precious to God. Read Isaiah 43:4 out loud. What three words does the prophet use to describe God's feelings toward His people?

- Most of us find it hard to reconcile these two truths: 1) I am precious to God, yet 2) He allows hardship and pain. In such times, you can cling to the words of Isaiah: "When you pass through the waters, I will be with you; and when you pass through the rivers, they will not sweep over you. When you walk through the fire, you will not be burned; the flames will not set you ablaze" (43:2). What is your "personalized version" of this verse (see page 26 in this book)?

Day 4: I AM ACCEPTED BY GOD

- While many of us have experienced rejection and some of us have been scorned by someone who should have loved us, the Word of God says we are totally and completely accepted by our heavenly Father (Ephesians 1:3-10). What does Psalm 27:10 teach us about this kind of acceptance? What does Jeremiah 31:3 say to you personally?

- Are there times you struggle with feeling accepted by God? What causes those doubts? What can you do to be assured of His acceptance?

Day 5: I AM CALLED BY NAME BY GOD

- Read the following quote by Charles Haddon Spurgeon: "He who counts the stars, and calls them by their names, is in no danger of forgetting His own children. He knows you as thoroughly as if you were the only creature He ever made, or the only saint He ever loved." How important is it to know a person by name? How do you feel when you think about God knowing you by name?

- Psalm 139:13-16 makes it clear we are intimately known by God. What truths are expressed in these verses?

Day 6: I AM BAPTIZED WITH CHRIST

- The apostle Paul said that Christians have been "baptized into Christ" (Romans 6:3). What does this phrase mean to you? (Note: The word *baptize* means to immerse. Hence the symbolism of total immersion in water baptism. The spiritual "baptism" that takes place at the moment of salvation is a work of the Holy Spirit placing you "in Christ." You are totally and permanently identified with Him—immersed in Him. Being lowered or baptized into physical water is a symbol of being identified with the death and burial of Jesus. Being raised up out of the water is a symbol of being identified with the new resurrection life of Jesus.)

- Read aloud one of the personalized verses related to baptism in Christ (see page 32 of the book).

Day 7: I Am Hidden with Christ

- In this day's reading, we learn about Corrie ten Boom's family providing a hiding place for the Jews who were being persecuted and put to death. Similarly, God has promised His children a "hiding place" (Psalm 32:7). What does this phrase mean to you?

- The idea of God providing a hiding place for His children is more than just poetic language. What are some practical ways to find safety and shelter in the Lord?

Days 8-15
God's Plan for Me

"'Come now, let us reason together,' says the LORD. 'Though your sins are like scarlet, they shall be as white as snow; though they are red as crimson, they shall be like wool'"
(ISAIAH 1:18).

In Luke 15:11-31, Jesus told the story of a rebellious son who demanded his inheritance before his father's death. He was tired of living under his father's roof, restricted by his rules. "Give me the share of property that is coming to me," he said.

The father did as his son asked. Soon the boy took all he had and left for a distant country. Naturally, that is not what the father wanted for his son. He understood the dangers and hardships awaiting him. As he watched the boy walk away, it would be reasonable to say the father's own "plan" for his son's life had not worked out too well.

Sure enough, the son quickly squandered everything he had on reckless living. Then the new country in which he lived experienced a terrible famine. The only work the boy could find was feeding livestock. He was so destitute and so wretched he just wished to be fed along with the pigs he was feeding (to Jews, pigs were unclean animals, so this would have been a detestable act). He could sink no lower. The bright future his father no doubt planned for him was completely ruined.

One day the rebel son came to his senses and realized his mistakes. He made up his mind to return home and ask for forgiveness…even if it meant living as a servant in a place where he had once enjoyed the full privileges of a son.

The end of the story is well known. When the father saw his son coming over the horizon, he was filled with joy and literally ran to meet him in the fields. Not only did the father place a fine robe on his son's shoulders and a ring on his finger, he also ordered a huge feast in celebration. And he proudly proclaimed, "For this son of mine was... lost and is found" (Luke 15:24).

Despite all that had happened, the father's ultimate "plan" for his son—to love him unconditionally and forgive him freely when he returned—never wavered for an instant.

God also has an unshakable plan for each of us: to lead us to repentance, redeem us from sin, reconcile us to Himself, and make us full-fledged sons and daughters in His house forever. When we rebel, His plan is the same. When we wander, His plan is the same. His heart rejoices when we approach Him. In our darkest hour, God's perfect plan points the way home.

Day 8: I Am Chosen by God

- When people become Christians, they sometimes say, "I accepted Christ" or "I asked Jesus to come into my heart." However, Scripture teaches that long before you made an initial decision to follow Jesus, God chose *you* (read John 15:16 and Ephesians 1:4). He chose you not because of your good qualities or strengths, but simply because He loved you. He wanted you. Think about this truth for a moment. How does it make you feel? How could this truth impact your daily life?

- Have you had the experience of being chosen for something important (a job, a sport, a play, or to be a speaker or a soloist)? If so, it probably felt wonderful. Now consider being chosen by the God of the universe to be His child. What thoughts and feelings come to mind? How does being chosen by God influence the way you think about yourself?

Day 9: I Am Born Again by God

- When God created Adam and Eve, they were made in his own image (Genesis 1:27), and they enjoyed oneness of mind and heart. When Adam and Eve sinned, how did it affect them spiritually? What consequences did it have on all who were born after them? (Note: Their sin was the seeking after self-sufficiency: They ate of the fruit of the tree of the knowledge of good and evil so they wouldn't have to depend on God for that knowledge. God allowed them to pursue self-sufficiency, but in so doing, they lost their intimacy with Him. Since that time, all of us have struggled with the desire to be in control of our own lives. It is only when we come to the point of understanding the futility of living a self-sufficient lifestyle that we seek after God.)

- The term *born again* has been distorted by the media and other who want it to be associated with "religious nuts" or "narrow-minded zealots." But what is the true, biblical meaning of the term *born again?* Explain what being born again means as it applies to you.

Day 10: I Am Saved by God

- Not only are we *chosen* by God and *born again* into the family of God, but we are also *saved*. What does the word *saved* mean? What are we "saved" from? (Describe what is included in the scope of our salvation—past, present, and future implications.)

- What does Hebrews 7:25 teach us about salvation?

Day 11: I Am Justified by God

- Ask a group member to explain what is meant by *justification*. What is the difference between being pardoned and being justified? (Note: To be pardoned means the penalty for our sins has already been paid. That was the purpose of the shedding of Jesus' blood. However, pardon still recognizes our guilt. Justification declares we are innocent. By the blood of Jesus, not only are our sins *forgiven*, but we are also *cleansed* from all unrighteousness.)

- Read Romans 5:1-2. What are some of the results of being justified?

Day 12: I Am Redeemed by God

- What does the word *redeemed* mean? How does this definition apply to your spiritual life?

- Read one of the personalized passages about redemption (on page 46 in the book).

Day 13: I Am Forgiven by God

- Read 1 John 1:9. What does this verse teach about God's love and grace?

- Why do so many Christians struggle with guilt feelings even though God promises complete forgiveness? What are some practical ways to receive and experience the Lord's grace?

Day 14: I Am Washed by God

- In everyday language, what does it mean to be "washed by God"?

- Ask: In what ways does God's grace and power provide us with a fresh, new start? How does the cleansing by God's Spirit enable us to move forward with confidence and conviction? In what ways do you need a fresh start?

Day 15: I Am Reconciled by God

- Whenever we experience a broken relationship (especially involving a close friend or family member), our hearts long for *reconciliation*. The original New Testament Greek word for reconciled means "to change thoroughly, to exchange from one condition to another." According to Romans 5:10, why do we need to be reconciled to God? How does this process of reconciliation happen in your spiritual life? (Note: The condition of the unbeliever is that of being an enemy to God. The sin of seeking self-sufficiency means we are rebels against God and therefore enemies of His will for us. For us to be reconciled to Him, this condition has to be radically altered. This supernatural change was accomplished by the death of Jesus as the sacrifice for our sins—a sacrifice we were incapable of making ourselves.)

- In what ways are the words *reconcile* or *reconciliation* used in our human relationships? How is this similar and different from the biblical use?

Days 16-23
My Possessions in Christ

"He gives strength to the weary and increases the power of the weak. Even youths grow tired and weary, and young men stumble and fall; but those who hope in the LORD will renew their strength. They will soar on wings like eagles; they will run and not grow weary, they will walk and not be faint"

(ISAIAH 40:29-31).

Throughout history and in every culture, if human beings have one thing in common, it might be this: *our fear of not having enough.* The constant desire for "things" can cost sleepless nights of worry, scheming how to get ahead in life. Making possessions a priority has caused nations to fight ruinous wars over "scarce" resources.

This same fear is also found in Christians who live with a constant sense of inadequacy in their walk with God. They often see themselves as empty-handed, utterly ill-equipped to handle what life throws at them. I assure you, this is *not* how God sees us—ever.

In the Sermon on the Mount, Jesus confronted this debilitating fear head-on when He said, "Do not worry about your life, what you will eat or what you will drink, nor about your body, what you will wear. Is not life more than food, and the body more than clothes?" (Matthew 6:25).

That's easier said than done!

Which is why the Lord tells us to compare ourselves to the birds and the flowers. They don't labor and fret, yet God feeds them and clothes them with beauty. His message is clear: It is absurd to think He will not also do the same for us.

But these examples run even deeper than food and clothing. If we truly "consider" a sparrow, for instance, we see how God does more than simply feed it. The bird is outfitted with everything needed to survive and thrive. Its feathers provide warmth and allow it to fly. Its beak is ideally suited for cracking seeds and building nests. Even its song serves to attract a mate or warn its young. In other words, the little sparrow lacks nothing. It's perfect just as it is…at peace in the hands of God.

And it's the same for you when you've trusted your life to the Creator. The apostle Paul wrote in Philippians 4:19, "My God will meet all your needs according to His glorious riches in Christ Jesus." Not *some* needs…not *most* needs…but *every* need. Therefore, it's time to put aside the fear of lack, for in Jesus, we already possess everything we need to live the abundant life God promises us.

Day 16: I Am Given a New Heart by God

- Jeremiah 17:9 describes the human heart as being "deceitful above all things" and "beyond cure." From the very beginning of our lives, our hearts have been self-seeking and self-serving. In light of this self-centered condition, Ezekiel 36:26 offers hope. What does this verse promise?

- When God changes a person's heart, there is healing, freedom and hope for the future. When the apostle Paul wrote to his young protégé Timothy, he listed some evidences of a new heart. What are some of these characteristics as found in 1 Timothy 1:5 and 2 Timothy 2:22?

Day 17: I Am Given the Spirit of God

- God designed the human spirit to be filled and controlled by the Holy Spirit of God. What are some of the roles He plays in our life? (Read Ephesians 1:13; John 16:13; Luke 12:12; John 14:26; Romans 5:5; Romans 14:7; 1 Corinthians 6:19; 2 Peter 1:21.)

- Read Galatians 5:22-25 out loud. With these "fruit of the Spirit" in mind, what do you think God's purpose is in giving us His Spirit? How does He accomplish this?

Day 18: I Am Given Everything I Need by God

- Our heavenly Father has opened a bank account in our name with deposits beyond our ability to exhaust. What are some of the resources available to us?

- In your own words, define the difference between what you *need* to live the Christian life—the life you were called to live—and what you merely *want* in regard to earthly desires.

Day 19: I Am Given Strength from God

- God promises to give "strength to the weary" and to increase the "power of the weak" (Isaiah 40:29). According to the verses on page 62, what is the source of our strength? How much strength is provided? Is this an external strength or an inner strength?

- Most people call on God for strength during times of trial or trauma. What strategies can you think of that might help you learn to lean on His strength when you're *not* in the midst of a trauma or trial?

Day 20: I Am Given the Mercy of God

- Jesus showed mercy to the woman caught in the sin of adultery. One definition of mercy is "active compassion." Under what circumstances does God extend such mercy? (Note: His mercy is confined only by the willingness of a person to repent and to receive His mercy. See Lamentations 3:22-25 for additional insight.)

- Can you recall a situation in your life when you expected justice, but instead God granted mercy? Would you be willing to share your experience?

Day 21: I Am Given the Grace of God

- Because of God's grace we are set free from living defeated lives. What did Paul say about God's grace in 2 Corinthians 12:9 and in 1 Timothy 1:14?

- Have you ever experienced failure and received an extra measure of God's grace? Would you be willing to share your experience?

Day 22: I Am Given Complete Access to God

- Because of our relationship with Christ, we have complete access to God and may approach Him "with freedom and confidence" (Ephesians 3:12). How did you personalize Hebrews 4:16 (page 68 in the book)?

- Are there things in your own life you never take to God in prayer because you secretly believe they are too small or petty? Do you think God shares that attitude?

Day 23: I Am Given the Mind of Christ

- The apostle Paul wrote regarding believers, "We have the mind of Christ" (1 Corinthians 2:16). What do you think it means to have the "mind" of Christ? Have you seen this truth at work in your own life? Give an example.

- In a computer, dozens of unseen programs run behind the scenes of what you see on your monitor. What invisible programs (thoughts and beliefs) are running in your mind that you would like to replace with the mind of Christ? How would your life change if you did?

Section 4

Days 24-31
God's Purpose for Me

"His divine power has given us everything we need
for life and godliness through our knowledge of him
who called us by his own glory and goodness"

(2 PETER 1:3).

Why am I on earth? Does God have a purpose for me? How do I find it?

These questions we have in common...and we have asked them at different times in our lives, more than once. As a believer, you want to serve God with all your heart. But how? Sometimes the answer seems to hover just out of reach over the horizon like a shimmering mirage in the desert.

In reality, the truth is not hidden at all. Jesus answered the question as plainly as possible one day when a lawyer, hoping to trick Him, asked which was the greatest of all God's commandments. The man thought he had handed Jesus a hopelessly tangled theological knot. Christ, of course, was ready.

"Love the Lord your God with all your heart and with all your soul and with all your mind. This is the great and first commandment. And the second is like it: Love your neighbor as yourself" (Matthew 22:37-39).

In other words, *love* is always at the center of God's purpose for you—love and devotion first to the Lord, and then love and service flowing outward to each other. If you live each day in the single-minded pursuit of these two commandments, you will never stray an inch from His will for your life. It is through you—despite all your doubts and imperfections—that God intends to pour out His living water on the earth and draw all who are thirsty to Him.

Helen Keller once said, "Believe, when you are most unhappy, that there is something for you to do in the world. So long as you can sweeten another's pain, life is not in vain."

Love God. Love each other. God's purpose for you really is that simple.

Day 24: I Am Created to Do Good Works for Christ

- Before you or I became a child of God, He had already prepared meaningful work for us to do. No matter how insignificant certain tasks may seem to be, they are never too small in God's sight. How do your attitudes about your calling help or hinder God's purpose for you?

- Read aloud James 2:14-26. Why is it so important to express your faith as "works" in the world?

Day 25: I Am an Ambassador for Christ

- Ephesians 4:1 encourages believers to "live a life worthy of the calling you have received." You are called to be an ambassador for Christ. What is an ambassador? How does a Christian function as an ambassador in the world?

- Read Ephesians 6:19-20 out loud. Even though Paul was imprisoned, was he still an ambassador for Christ? What did he ask the Ephesian Christians to do for him? What did Paul say about their calling in life?

Day 26: I Am Being Conformed to Christ

- In addition to the work God has planned for you to do, His purpose for your life includes the development of Christian character. He says you are predestined "to be conformed to the likeness of his Son" (Romans 8:29). In your own words, what does this mean?

- According to Romans 12:2, what is also required? What are some practical ways people can renew their minds?

Day 27: I Am Complete in Christ

- Your human heart yearns to be connected with someone significant—someone who will make you feel complete. Yet the Bible says we are "complete in Him" (Colossians 2:10 NKJV). In light of the loneliness we all experience from time to time, what has Jesus promised?

- Most people strive to feel "complete" by acquiring external things: possessions, money, status, relationships. How would your life be different if you suddenly stopped struggling and accepted that you are already completely whole in Christ?

Day 28: I Am Clothed with the Righteousness of Christ

- Righteousness is a state of being forgiven and cleansed of sin. It is also a quality of specific behavior. With this in mind, what do you think it means to be "clothed" in righteousness (Job 29:14)?

- Do you think righteousness is a garment we can ever weave for ourselves?

Day 29: I Am Holy Before God

- Read 1 Peter 1:15-16. How would you define *holiness?* (Note: Holiness is being totally set apart, totally different, totally other.) God is not an "improved" version of who we are. He is totally different; He is holy. He has called and equipped us also to be holy—different from what we were, different from the world, and set apart for His purposes.

- We are set apart to live holy lives. Based on your experience, how is this possible?

Day 30: I Am Safe in the Protection of God

- Like a parent who is ready to catch a toddler learning to walk, our heavenly Father is always prepared to offer help, support, and safety. What does Romans 8:31 say about this idea?

- Do you believe God's promise of protection means you will never face hard times? If not, why?

Day 31: I Am Secure in the Love of God

- Were you ever hurt by someone in a relationship that was *not* secure and loving? Is it hard for you to trust others as a result? Do you find it hard to trust God's love as well?

- Mention as many words as possible to describe God's love (unconditional, everlasting, unfathomable, forgiving, freeing, and so on). Identify which of these aspects of God's love is most meaningful to you personally. Why?

Congratulations on completing the *Seeing Yourself Through God's Eyes* devotional study! My prayer is that, over these last few weeks, you have gained life-changing insights into your *position, plan, possessions,* and *purpose* in Christ.

While you have *completed* the study, the journey of *applying* these precious truths in your daily life—for the *rest* of your life—is just beginning! I encourage you to continue meditating on each of the 31 "I am" statements found in the study. Such review will enable you to absorb God's view of you more deeply into your heart—furthering the "spiritual soaking" that has already begun.

May you be blessed—and be a great blessing to others—as you see yourself through God's eyes!

Notes

1. Maxwell Maltz, *Psycho-Cybernetics: A New Way to Get More Out of Life* (New York: Pocket Books, 1960), 109.

2. Thomas Watson, *Body of Divinity Contained in Sermons Upon the Assembly's Cateckism* (London: Passmore & Alabaster, 1881), 163.

3. Jeremy Taylor, *The Whole Works of the Right Rev. Jeremy Taylor with an Essay Biographical and Critical,* vol. 1 (London: Henry G. Bohn, 1851), 820.

4. Anna B. Warner, *Jesus Loves Me,* first published in 1859.

5. Charles H. Spurgeon, *Morning and Evening: Daily Readings* (Lynchburg, VA: The Old-Time Gospel Hour, n.d.), 111.

6. E.Y. Harburg, *Over the Rainbow* (n.p.: n.p., 1938).

7. Corrie ten Boom, John L. Sherrill, and Elizabeth Sherrill, *The Hiding Place* (Washington Depot, CT: Chosen, 1971), 192-93.

8. William Orcutt Cushing, *Under His Wings,* date of writing and publication unknown.

9. Lawrence Richards, *Expository Dictionary of Bible Words,* electronic ed. (Grand Rapids: Zondervan, 1985).

10. James L. Nicholson, "Whiter Than Snow," in *Joyful Songs No. 4* (Philadelphia: Methodist Episcopal Book Room, 1872).

11. William J. Kirkpatrick, *Lord I'm Coming Home,* in *Winning Songs* (Philadelphia: John J. Hood, 1892).

12. Annie J. Flint, *He Giveth More Grace,* Casterline Card Series, no. 5510 (Oxford Park, NY: n.p., n.d.).

13. A.W. Tozer, *The Pursuit of God* (Camp Hill, PA: Christian, 1993), 127.

14. Frank Hobbs and Nicole Stoops, *Demographic Trends in the 20th Century: Census 2000 Special Reports,* Series CENSR-4 (Washington, DC: U.S. Government Printing Office, 2002), 2.

15. This world record was set in 2005.

16. Frederick M. Lehman, *The Love of God,* in *Songs That Are Different,* vol. 2 (n.p.: n.p., 1919).

About the Author

June Hunt is founder and CEO of **Hope For The Heart** (www.HopeForTheHeart .org) and is a dynamic Christian leader who has yielded landmark contributions to the field of Christian counseling. Hope For The Heart provides biblically based counsel in 24 languages and has worked in 60 countries on six continents. June, who celebrated 25 years of ministry in 2011, is also an author, speaker, musician, and has served as guest professor to a variety of colleges and seminaries.

Early family pain shaped June's heart of compassion. Her bizarre family background left her feeling hopeless and caused June to contemplate "drastic solutions." But when June entered into a life-changing relationship with Jesus Christ, the trajectory of her life was forever altered. As a result, she grew passionate about helping people face life's tough circumstances.

As a youth director, June became aware of the need for real answers to real questions. Her personal experiences with pain and her practical experience with youth and parents led June into a lifelong commitment to *Providing God's Truth for Today's Problems*. She earned a master's in counseling at Criswell College in 2007 and has been presented with two honorary doctorates.

Between 1989 and 1992, June Hunt developed and taught *Counseling Through the Bible*, a scripturally based counseling course addressing 100 topics in categories such as marriage and family, emotional entrapments and cults, as well as addictions, abuse, and apologetics. Since then, the coursework has been continuously augmented and refined, forming the basis for the *Biblical Counseling Library*. Her *Biblical Counseling Keys* became the foundation of the ministry's expansion, including the 2002 creation of the *Hope Biblical Counseling Institute* (BCI) initiated by Criswell College to equip spiritual leaders, counselors, and people with hearts to help others with practical solutions for life's most pressing problems.

The *Biblical Counseling Keys* provide a foundation for the ministry's two daily radio programs, *Hope For The Heart* and *Hope In The Night*, both hosted by June. *Hope For The Heart* is a half-hour of interactive teaching heard on over 100 radio outlets across America, and *Hope In The Night* is June's live two-hour call-in counseling program. Together, both programs air domestically and internationally on more than 1000 stations. In 1986, the National Religious Broadcasters (NRB) honored *Hope For The Heart* as "Best New Radio Program" and awarded it Radio Program of the Year in 1989. Women in Christian Media presented June Hunt with an Excellence in Communications award in 2008. The ministry received NRB's Media Award for International Strategic Partnerships in 2010.

As an accomplished musician, June has been a guest on numerous national TV and radio programs, including NBC's *Today*. She has toured overseas with the USO and has been a guest soloist at Billy Graham Crusades. June communicates her message of hope on five music recordings: *The Whisper of My Heart*, *Hymns of Hope*, *Songs of Surrender*, *Shelter Under His Wings*, and *The Hope of Christmas*.

June Hunt's numerous books include *Seeing Yourself Through God's Eyes*, *How to Forgive...When You Don't Feel Like It*, *Counseling Through Your Bible Handbook*, *How to Handle Your Emotions*, *How to Rise Above Abuse*, *Bonding with Your Teen through Boundaries*, *Keeping Your Cool...When Your Anger Is Hot*, *Caring for a Loved One with Cancer* (June is a cancer survivor), and *Hope for Your Heart: Finding Strength in Life's Storms*. She is also a contributor to the *Soul Care Bible* and the *Women's Devotional Bible*.

June Hunt resides in Dallas, Texas, home of the international headquarters of Hope For The Heart.

Other Harvest House Books
by June Hunt

The Biblical Counseling Reference Guide

Everyone faces difficulties. And God gave us the Bible so that we would have the answers we need to resolve them. In an instant, this powerful resource helps you to find thousands of Bible verses related to over 580 practical, everyday issues—all in one volume.

Counseling Through Your Bible Handbook

The Bible is richly relevant when it comes to the difficult dilemmas of life. Here are 50 chapters of spiritual wisdom and compassionate counsel on issues such as anger, adultery, depression, fear, guilt, grief, rejection, and self-worth.

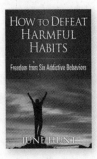

How to Defeat Harmful Habits

Addictions are powerful. How can you help a friend, loved one, or even yourself find freedom? This book of expert direction and gripping real-life stories demonstrates that with God, all things really are possible, including lasting freedom from even the most destructive addictions.

How to Handle Your Emotions

In Scripture, God gives counsel that helps us process our full range of emotions in a healthy way. Learn how to better navigate your emotions by understanding their definitions, characteristics, and causes, as well as the solutions that lead to emotional growth.

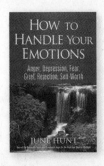

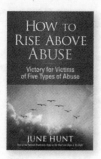

How to Rise Above Abuse

Compassionate, practical, hands-on guidance for the toughest issues to talk about—childhood sexual abuse, spiritual abuse, verbal and emotional abuse, victimization, and wife abuse. Filled with the hope and healing only Christ can give.

How to Forgive… When You Don't Feel Like It

Though we know God has called us to forgive, we find ourselves asking hard questions: What if it hurts too much to forgive? What if the other person isn't sorry? How can I let someone off the hook for doing something so wrong? If you've been struggling with resentment or bitterness, here's how to find true freedom through forgiveness.

The Answer to Anger

This book explores the causes and kinds of anger and the biblical steps toward resolution. You will learn how to identify the triggers of anger, ways of dealing with past angers, what the Bible says about righteous and unrighteous anger, and how to bring about real and lasting change.